Historic Michigan Travel Guide

5ᵗʰ Edition

Larry J. Wagenaar
Emily E. Asbenson

An official publication of the

Sponsored by:

Rollin M. Gerstacker Foundation

The Historical Society of Michigan
Lansing

Contents

Introduction

Michigan is a state with rich cultural and heritage resources. Against that backdrop, the state's history museums, historic sites, and other destinations tell the story of our past. A walk through Michigan's history will lead you to unique opportunities in some of the most interesting places you can visit in the Great Lakes State.

As you explore this new edition of the *Historic Michigan Travel Guide,* you will find opportunities to go underground on a mine tour in the Copper Country of the Upper Peninsula or see where Ford's Model T was constructed in Detroit. Whether you are visiting large institutions such as the Public Museum of Grand Rapids or smaller facilities like the Les Cheneaux Historical and Maritime Museums in Cedarville, the *Historic Michigan Travel Guide* will provide you with key information you need to know, including location, operating hours, admission fees, highlights of exhibits and collections, and more.

With the explosive growth of cultural and heritage tourism in recent years and the renewed interest in having a simple, easy-to-use guide to finding those resources, the Historical Society of Michigan is committed to bringing Michigan citizens and our visitors this useful tool, which is revised and published triennially.

All of the museums and other history destinations included in this guide are organizational members of the Historical Society of Michigan. If your local institution or one you visit is not included, it can ensure placement in the next edition by joining the Society. The Historical Society of Michigan is not a part of state government (we are a 501(c)(3) educational organization), and we rely on members to undertake our programming, including the publication of this guide. Inclusion in the *Historic Michigan Travel Guide* is one of the many benefits of membership for history organizations.

Finally, we encourage you to consider personal membership in the Historical Society of Michigan. Among our offerings is the award-winning *Michigan History* magazine, our quarterly membership magazine the Chronicle, the *Michigan Historical Review* journal, and much more. It is an excellent way to stay connected to Michigan's heritage. See the rear pages of this guide for more information on the many benefits and opportunities available to members of the state historical society.

www.hsmichigan.org

Acknowledgments

The new 5th Edition of the *Historic Michigan Travel Guide* could not have come together without the help of our key sponsors, members of the Historical Society of Michigan (HSM) staff, our Board of Trustees, and the hundreds of organizations that submitted information to the Historical Society of Michigan for inclusion.

One of our leading Michigan-based retailers—Meijer—provided financial support as well as distribution in all of its Michigan stores to make this new edition of the *Historic Michigan Travel Guide* widely available. Grants from the Huizenga Group and the Rollin M. Gerstacker Foundation also provided critical help to bring this publication together. Together their support made it possible to do the extensive work of collecting the necessary data, revising our database systems, writing, editing, typesetting, and publishing.

The *Historic Michigan Travel Guide* builds on the work we do triennially on a companion reference volume, the *Michigan History Directory*. The *Directory* documents more than 800 historical organizations of all types throughout its pages. The next edition will be published in fall 2011. Unlike the *Travel Guide*, however, organizational membership in HSM is not required to be listed in the *Directory*. The data provided by local organizations for the *Directory* and the *Travel Guide*—and the efforts of HSM staff past and present that have worked on it—was also critical in assembling the information for this guide.

Several individuals assisted with various tasks including copyediting of the text. We would like to thank *Michigan History* Editor Patricia Majher, HSM Assistant Director Shannon White, and the staff of the Historical Society of Michigan and its subsidiary, *Michigan History* magazine, for their assistance.

Larry J. Wagenaar
Executive Director, The Historical Society of Michigan
Publisher, Michigan History Magazine L3C

About the Listings

Each of the entries in this guide provides helpful information to enable you to contact, visit, and enjoy these historic Michigan sites.

Requirements

To be included in the *Historic Michigan Travel Guide* the historic destination must be a member of the Historical Society of Michigan (HSM) and must allow public access.

Organization

The listings are divided into two major groups based on our state's geography. Upper Peninsula destinations are listed first (pages 9-28) followed by Lower Peninsula listings (pages 29-112). Community names are ordered alphabetically with an alphabetic list of their sites following. Multiple locations maintained by one organization within the same community are listed together.

Information

The following information, in whole or in part, was provided to us by each site:

1. Name of the historic destination

2. Physical location of the site

3. Contact information including telephone, e-mail, and website

4. Mailing address (if other than site location)

5. Public hours

6. Admission fee

7. Site information including parking, access, and guide availability

8. Annual events

9. Description of the site and its attractions

Upper Peninsula

Brimley

Wheels of History Museum Train

Location: 6799 S. M-221, Brimley, MI 49715.
Contact: (906) 437-5560, www.baymillsbrimleyhistory.org.
Mail: P.O. Box 273. *Hours:* Mid-May to mid-Oct 10am-4pm.
Admission: Free. *Site Info:* Street parking. Not wheelchair accessible.
Guides available. *Events:* 4th of July Celebration.
Wheels of History Museum Train, administered by the Bay Mills
Brimley Historical Research Society, is a wooden caboose passenger car
with six major display cases highlighting the railroad in Brimley, Bay
Mills townsite, mining and logging, and Lake Superior fishing and
fishing boats.

Calumet

Coppertown USA Mining Museum

Location: 25815 Red Jacket Rd., Calumet, MI 49913.
Contact: (906) 337-2303, (906) 337-4354,
www.uppermichigan.com/coppertown. *Mail:* 56638 Calumet Ave.
Hours: Jun-Sep Mon-Sat 11am-5 pm. *Admission:* Adults $3, youth (12-
18) $1, children (under 12) free. *Site Info:* Free parking. Wheelchair
accessible. Introductory video & self-guided tour, guided tour for groups
by appointment. *Events:* Calumet Heritage Days Open House.
Museum features 100 displays, dating back to the 19th century in the
former Calumet and Hecla Pattern shop, that introduce the fascinating
story of the Copper Country and America's first mining boom.
Attractions include a copper knife from Copper Culture Indians, 13-
minute Keweenaw copper video, simulated mine shaft, railroad
memorabilia, shoe shop, and old school exhibits. A Heritage Site of the
Keweenaw National Historical Park.

Keweenaw National Historical Park

Location: 25970 Red Jacket Rd., Calumet, MI 49913.
Contact: (906) 337-3168, brian_hoduski@nps.gov, www.nps.gov/kewe.
Mail: P.O. Box 471. *Hours:* Mon-Fri 9am-5pm. *Admission:* Free.

Site Info: Free parking. Self-guided.

The Historical Park consists of two locations that are 12 miles apart in Calumet and Quincy, once the homes of two large mines that were prominent in the community. The Quincy mine presents the process that was required for the cultivation of the area's minerals. The Calumet mine represents the social and cultural effects the mine company had on the area. Visitors will find remnants of life during one of the country's first mineral rushes including period buildings. Area historical organizations partner to preserve the heritage of copper mining through original structures and landscapes of the copper era. The information desk at Quincy Mine is open during the summer.

Norwegian Lutheran Church
Location: 338 7th St., Calumet, MI 49913.
Contact: (906) 337-3731, www.nlc-calumet.org. *Mail:* 608 Elm St.
Hours: Jun-Oct daily 9am-5pm. *Admission:* By donation. *Site Info:* Free street parking. Not wheelchair accessibile. Guided tours during Calumet Heritage Days (Aug).

The Norwegian Lutheran Church Historical Society was founded in 2000 to restore and maintain this historic former Church building. Church contains original altar, pews, organ, chandelier, and tin ceiling.

Caspian

Iron County Historical Museum
Location: Brady St. at Museum Rd., Caspian, MI 49915.
Contact: (906) 265-2617, ironcountymuseum@sbcglobal.net, www.ironcountymuseum.com.
Mail: P.O. Box 272. *Hours:* Mid-May to Oct Mon-Sat 9am-5pm, Sun 1-5pm.
Admission: Adults $7, Youth (5-18) $2.50. *Site Info:* Free parking. Partially wheelchair accessible. Self-guided.
Events: West Iron County Student Art Show, Scandinavian Heritage Day Celebration, Ferrous Frolics, Lee LeBlanc Dinner, Iron County Fine Arts Show, Hobby & Collections Show, Pie Social, Christmas Tree Galleria, St. Lucia Breakfast.

Founded in 1962, the grounds of the Caspian Mine include a headframe and engine house converted to a museum. The 8½ acre site includes a log cabin homesite, lumber camp, mine site, Victorian area with the Carrie Jacobs Bond Home, 500-seat Cultural Center, and 3 galleries including the LeBlanc Wildlife Art Gallery. The museum's 75 displays include mining, lumbering (80-ft Monigal Miniature Lumber Camp), shops, pioneer home, and carver's room.

Cedarville

Les Cheneaux Historical and Maritime Museums
Location: 105 S. Meridian Rd., Cedarville, MI 49719.
Contact: (906) 484-2821, lcha@cedarville.net, www.lchistorical.org.
Mail: P.O. Box 301. *Hours:* Memorial Day weekend to mid-Sep Tue-Sat 10am-4 pm, Sun 1-4pm, also by appointment. *Admission:* Individual $2, Family $5, 12 & under free. *Site Info:* Free parking. Historical Museum is wheelchair accessible, Maritime Museum is partially accesssible. Self-guided. *Events:* Antique Wooden Boat Show and Festival of Arts (Aug).
Maintained by the Les Cheneaux Historical Association, the Historical Museum, founded in 1968, displays highlight Indian crafts, logging era tools, model of a lumber camp, early settlers and the hotel and tourist periods. The Maritime Museum in the 1920s O.M. Reif Boathouse displays vintage boats, marine artifacts, antique outboard motors, historic photos, and a boat-building workshop.

Chassell

Chassell Heritage Center

Location: 42373 Hancock St., Chassell, MI 49916.
Contact: (906) 523-1155, nancy@einerlei.com, www.einer lei.com/community/CHO.html.
Mail: P.O. Box 331. *Hours:* Jul-Aug Tue 1-4pm, Thurs 4-9pm.
Admission: Donations accepted.
Site Info: Free on-site parking. Not wheelchair accessible. Guides available. *Events:* Special Summer Evening Programs, Strawberry Festival Open House (Jul), Old Fashioned Christmas Open House (Dec).
The Heritage Center, administered by the Chassell Historical Organization, is located in a former elementary school with exhibits including local strawberry farming, the Old School, vintage clothing, and a township timeline.

Copper Harbor

Copper Harbor Lighthouse
Location: By boat from Copper Harbor Marina, Fort Wilkins State Park, Copper Harbor, MI 49918.
Contact: (906) 475-7857, (906) 289-4215, friggenst@michigan.gov, www.copperharborlighthouse.com, www.michigan.gov/fortwilkins.
Mail: P.O. Box 71. *Hours:* Call for current hours and fees. *Site Info:* Free parking at Copper Harbor Marina, board boat to lighthouse. Lighthouse is not wheelchair accessible, 1849 Keeper's Dwelling is accessible with a virtual lighthouse tour. Call ahead for transportation

accommodation by DNRE staff. Boat captains transport tours from marina to site's self-guided exhibits.

Part of Fort Wilkins State Park, the lighthouse presents the duties and activities of a light keeper and his family set against the background of Lake Superior maritime history. The 1848 light keeper's dwelling serves as an orientation center for the site. Exhibits in the dwelling show why the light tower was built, how lights worked, who maintained light, and provide the overall context of the site.

Fort Wilkins Historic Complex

Location: Fort Wilkins State Park, 15223 US- 41, Copper Harbor, MI 49918.
Contact: (906) 475-7857, (906) 289-4215, friggenst@michigan.gov, www.michigan.gov/ftwilkins.
Mail: P.O. Box 71.
Hours: Museum Mid-May to mid-Oct daily 8am-dusk. Business office Mon-Fri 8am-4:30pm. *Admission:* Michigan State Park Motor Vehicle Permit required. *Site Info:* On-site parking. Partially wheelchair accessible. Self-guided with seasonal reenactment. *Events:* Fort Wilkins by Candlelight, Battery "D" Encampment, costumed reenactment (summer).

Built in 1844 on the shoreline of Lake Superior, the fort is a well-preserved example of mid-19th century army life. Site includes 19 buildings, 12 original from the 1840s, and the Pittsburgh and Boston mine site. Exhibits and programs interpret military life and the hardships of frontier isolation. Administered by the Michigan DNRE.

Covington

Covington Township Historical Museum

Location: Elm St., Covington, MI 49919.
Contact: (906) 355-2413, (906) 355-2573, marypt@jamadots.com, www.covingtonmi.com/historicalmuseum.aspx. *Mail:* P.O. Box 54.
Hours: Jun-Sep Thurs-Sun 10am-2pm. *Admission:* By donation.
Site Info: Street parking. Partially wheelchair accessible-first floor only. Guided tours available by donation. *Events:* Fall Festival, Monthly Film Nights.

Covington Historical Society, formed in 1997, maintains the museum in the former Township Hall. Exhibits include a horse-drawn cutter, military display, the first fire truck, and a jail cell used to house only one prisoner.

Crystal Falls

Harbour House Museum
Location: 17 N. 4th St., Crystal Falls, MI 49920.
Contact: (906) 875-4341, maryannh@up.net,
www.crystalfalls.org/harbour_house_museum.htm. *Mail:* P.O. Box 65.
Hours: Jun-Aug Tue-Sat 10am-2pm. *Admission:* Individual $3, Family
$5. *Site Info:* Street parking. Not wheelchair accessible. Docent
available. *Events:* Pie & Chili event (Sep), Harvest Festival.
Administered by the Crystal Falls Museum Society, the Harbour House
was built in 1900 for the Harbour family with offices for local attorney
and state legislator Michael Moriarty. Constructed with cement blocks
and designed in "steamboat" style architecture with wraparound twin
porches, the house is now a hands-on museum with activities during the
summer. Exhibit rooms include the Ojibwa Indian Room, Sports Room,
Veterans Room, and Children's Room and include mining, local history,
and family life artifacts.

Curtis

Curtis Historical Society Museum
Location: Portage Ave., Curtis, MI 49820.
Contact: (906) 586-3382, lakenyon@mich.com. *Mail:* P.O. Box 313.
Hours: Mon-Fri 1-4pm. *Admission:* Donations accepted. *Site Info:* On-
site parking. Wheelchair accessible. Self-guided.
This local history museum houses artifacts from early logging and
settlers. Exhibits include displays on school, military, and Native
Americans.

DeTour

DeTour Passage Historical Museum
Location: 104 Elizabeth St., DeTour Village, MI 49725.
Contact: rahudak39@yahoo.com. *Mail:* P.O. Box 111. *Hours:* Daily 1-
5pm. *Admission:* Free. *Site Info:* Street parking. Wheelchair accessible.
Events: Community Appreciation Days, Happy Apple Day.
A non-profit group formed to take possession of the lighthouse that
marks the DeTour Passage at the southern end of the St. Mary's River.
The DeTour Light was built in 1931 at the end of the DeTour Reef, 1
mile from shore at its nearest point. Artifacts include a Fresnel lens from
the reef lighthouse, an old school bell, a military display, and many
photographs.

Eagle Harbor

Keweenaw County Historical Society Museums
Location: 670 Lighthouse Rd., Eagle Harbor, MI 49950.
Contact: (906) 289-4990, aboggio@pasty.com, vjamison@pasty.com, www.keweenawhistory.org.
A Heritage Site of the Keweenaw National Historical Park.

Eagle Harbor Lighthouse Complex
Hours: Jul-Aug Mon-Sat 10am-5pm. Jun, Sep, Oct Sun 12-5pm.
Admission: Adults $4.
Includes an 1887 light station, maritime museum, mining museum, and commercial fishing museum.

Rathbone School
Location: 200 Center St.
Hours: Open mid-Jun to Oct. *Admission:* By donation.
Exhibits presented in the restored 1853 Eagle Harbor School commemorate the birthplace of the Knights of Pythias, a fraternal order founded by Justus H. Rathbone in the 1860s.

Central Mine Village
Location: US-41 at Central Rd.
Hours: Visitor Center open in summer. *Admission:* By donation.
Events: Annual reunion of Central families' descendants (Jul).
Central Mine opened in 1854 and closed in 1898. The Society acquired the former company town in 1996.

Bammert Blacksmith Shop and Phoenix Church
Location: Corner of M-26 and US-41, Phoenix.
Hours: Mid-May to late Oct.
Features two restored buildings.

Engadine

Engadine Historical Museum
Location: W14075 Melville St., Engadine, MI 49827.
Contact: (906) 477-6908, (906) 293-4212,
deekaydee2000@sbcglobal.net. *Mail:* 6537 N. County Rd 403,
Newberry, MI 49868. *Hours:* Memorial Day-Sep Tue & Sat 10am-2pm.
Events: Heritage Day (Jul).
The museum reflects life in the community dating back to 1894, especially the lumber and agricultural eras, including furnishings, a one-room schoolhouse replica, and displays of military artifacts, pictures, and artifacts from the Cooperidge Mill and old Mackinac County Bank. Restored 1895 log house on property.

Escanaba

Delta County Historical Museum

Location: 16 Water Plant Rd., Escanaba, MI 49829.
Contact: (906) 789-6790, deltacountyhistsoc@sbcglobal.net, www.deltahistorical.org.
Hours: Museum/Lighthouse Memorial Day to Labor Day daily 11am-4pm. Archives
Jun-Aug Mon-Fri 1-4pm, Sep-May Mon 1-4pm. *Admission:* Adults $3, Children $1, Family $5. *Site Info:* Free parking. Museum is partially wheelchair accessible, Lighthouse is not. Self-guided.
The museum, begun in 1956 in a former radio station, features exhibits highlighting local history including domestic, commercial, athletic, and military heritage (including a fully restored surf boat). Lighthouse, home, tower, and boathouse are open; the home is furnished to circa 1900.

Garden

Fayette Historic Townsite
Location: Fayette Historic State Park, 13700 13.25 Ln., Garden, MI 49835.
Contact: (906) 644-2711, laaksob@michigan.gov, www.michigan.gov/fayette. *Hours:* May-Jun daily 9am-5pm, mid-Jun to Labor Day daily 9am-dusk, Labor Day-Oct daily 9am-5pm.
Admission: Michigan State Park Motor Vehicle Permit required.
Site Info: Free parking with entry permit. Partially wheelchair accessible: visitor center only. Self-guided, guided tours available during summer. *Events:* Fayette Heritage Day (Aug), Fall Fest (Oct).
Once a bustling industrial community that manufactured charcoal pig iron from 1867-1891. Modern visitor center, 20 historic structures, museum exhibits, and walking tours interpret Fayette's role as a company town. Administered by the Michigan DNRE.

Garden Peninsula Historical Museum
Location: State Rd M-183, Garden, MI 49835.
Contact: (906) 644-2398, cwilson@centurylink.net, www.hunts-upguide.com/garden_peninsula_detail.html. *Mail:* P.O. Box 93.
Hours: Memorial Day to Labor Day Wed-Sat 11am-3pm.
Admission: Free. *Site Info:* Street parking. Wheelchair accessible.
Events: Honoree dinner for area residents over 80 years old.
Administered by the Garden Peninsula Historical Society, the museum features artifacts and history of the Garden Peninsula and Big Bay de Noc logging, fishing, and farming industries.

Grand Marais

Lightkeeper's House Museum
Location: E. 22050 Coast Guard
Point Rd., Grand Marais, MI
49839
Contact: (906) 494-2404,
gmhistoricalsociety@gmail.com,
historicalsociety.grandmaraismichi
gan.com. *Mail:* P.O. Box 179.
Hours: All sites Jun & Sep

weekends 1-4pm, Jul-Aug daily 1-4pm. *Admission:* Donations accepted.
Site Info: On-site parking. Wheelchair accessible. Docent on-site.
Events: Plant Sale (May), Community Yard Sale (Jun), Silent Auction
(Jul).
The Grand Marais Historical Society operates the 1906 restored
residence of the Grand Marais Lightkeeper and a historic walking tour
of the village. The home is furnished with early 20th century pieces.

Old Post Office Museum and Memorial Rose Garden
Location: N. 14272 Lake Ave. *Site Info:* Street parking.
Wheelchair accessible. Self-guided.

Showcases the history of Grand Marais from early settlement to the
present day via exhibits on various eras of its history. A memorial
rose garden is located behind the museum.

Pickle Barrel House Museum and Historic Iris Garden
Location: N. 14252 Lake Ave. *Site Info:* Street parking. Not
wheelchair accessible. Docent on-site.

The Pickle Barrel House Museum is the restored cottage of
author/illustrator William Donahey, creator of the "Teeny Weenie"
cartoon characters. The Historic Iris Garden located on the property
features over 80 varieties of iris pre-dating 1935.

Hancock

Quincy Mine Hoist
Location: 49750 US-41, Hancock, MI 49930.
Contact: (906) 482-3101, (906) 482-5569, glenda@quincymine.com,
www.quincymine.com. *Hours:* May to mid-Jun Fri-Sun 9:30am-5pm,
mid-Jun to Oct daily 9:30am-5pm. *Admission:* Surface tour Adults &
Seniors $9.50, Youth $4.50. Full tour Adults $15, Seniors $14, Youth
$8. *Site Info:* On-site parking. Partially wheelchair accessible. Guided
tours.
Surface tours include visit to the museum in the No. 2 hoist building,
shaft house, and Norburg Steam Hoist, the world's largest steam engine.
Full tour includes a cog tram car to the mine and a wagon ride seven
levels underground. Exhibit from the Seaman Mineralogical Museum
includes a 17-ton solid copper boulder.

Hermansville

IXL Historical Museum

Location: W5561 River St.,
Hermansville, MI 49847.
Contact: (906) 498-2181,
museum@hermansville.com,
www.hermansville.com/IXL
Museum. *Mail:* P.O. Box 162.
Hours: Memorial Day to
Labor Day 12:30-4pm CDT.
Admission: $3.
Site Info: Street parking.
Partially wheelchair accessible

(outbuildings only). Guides and self-guided handbook available.
Events: Old Wheels Day & Quilt Show (Aug), Porcelain Doll Show.
Hermansville was the company town of Wisconsin Land and Lumber
Company, makers of IXL hardwood flooring. The museum in the
company's office building has many tools used in lumbering and mill
operations, lumbering artifacts, company records, and all records of
Blaney Park owned by the Wisconsin Land and Lumber Co. Photo
collection includes photos of the town, mill, lumbering camps, and
people who built the community.

Iron Mountain

Menominee Range Museum

Location: E. Ludington St., Iron Mountain, MI 49801.
Contact: (906) 774-4276, mrh-museum@sbcglobal.net,
www.menomineemuseum.com. *Mail:* P.O. Box 237. *Hours:* Memorial
Day-Oct Tue-Sat 10am-4pm, archives by appointment.
Admission: Adults $5, Seniors $4.50, Students $3. *Site Info:* Free
parking. Self-guided; for guided tours call (906) 774-1086.
The museum, begun in 1974 in the former 1901 Carnegie Library
building, has 100 displays telling the story of life on the Menominee
Iron Range.

Ironwood

Old Depot Museum

Location: 100 N. Lowell, Ironwood, MI 49938.
Contact: (906) 932-0287, twolees1@chartermi.net,
www.ironwoodmi.org/historical.htm. *Mail:* P.O. Box 553.
Hours: Memorial Day to Labor Day Mon-Sat 12-4pm. *Admission:* Free.
Site Info: Free parking. Wheelchair accessible. Free guides available.
Events: Festival Ironwood (Jul).
The Ironwood Area Historical Society maintains this museum in an
1892 depot shared with the Chamber of Commerce. Exhibits focus on

the history of Ironwood featuring the Gogebic Range, mining history and its significance to the area, and a general store as stocked in early Ironwood.

Ishpeming

U.S. Ski and Snowboard Hall of Fame

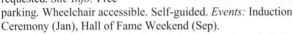

Location: 610 Palms Ave., Ishpeming, MI 49849.
Contact: (906) 485-6323, administrator@skihall.com, www.skihall.com. *Mail:* P.O. Box 191. *Hours:* Mon-Sat 10am-5pm.
Admission: Donations requested. *Site Info:* Free parking. Wheelchair accessible. Self-guided. *Events:* Induction Ceremony (Jan), Hall of Fame Weekend (Sep).

The only national museum in the UP, the Hall of Fame is dedicated to the preservation and promotion of America's ski and snowboarding heritage through recognition of nationally outstanding skiers and ski sport builders from the United States and through the preservation and presentation of sport artifacts and archives. Attractions include a theater, Honored Members Court, Olympic Tribute display, Tribute to the 10th Mountain Division, and America's first chair lift.

Kinross

Kinross Heritage Park

Location: 6277 W. M-80, Kinross, MI 49752.
Contact: (906) 478-3761, www.kinross.net. *Mail:* P.O. Box 34.
Hours: Thurs-Sun 1-5:30pm. *Admission:* Free. *Site Info:* Free parking (call ahead for buses or trailers). Museum & Log Cabin are wheelchair accessible. Free guide available. *Events:* Log Cabin Day (Jun), Fair Days, Annual Craft Show (Oct).

Kinross Heritage Society seeks to preserve the history of Kinross for future generations and administers the Heritage Park including an 1882 log cabin, 1902 one-room schoolhouse, working blacksmith shop, and early farming, household goods, and military displays. Quarter-mile nature trail on-site.

Lake Linden

Houghton County Museum
Location: 53150 M-26, Lake Linden, MI 49945.
Contact: (906) 296-4121, info@houghtonhistory.org,
www.houghtonhistory.org. *Mail:* P.O. Box 127. *Hours:* Museum Tue-Sun 12-4pm, Office Mon & Fri 9:30am-12pm. *Admission:* Adult $5,
Seniors & Students $3. *Site Info:* Free parking. Not wheelchair
accessible. Self-guided. *Events:* Train rides Sat-Sun 12-4pm.
The Houghton County Historical Society preserves, presents, and
interpets the history and culture of the Copper Country with emphasis on
Houghton County and copper mining. Exhibits include Lake Linden &
Torch Lake Railroad, a restored 0-4-0 Porter Steam Locomotive, and a
3' gauge track to support tours interpreting the former Calumet & Hecla
Mill. Trains run weekends. Site also houses a general history museum,
1940s WPA-constructed log cabin, schoolhouse, and the former 1st
Congregational Church of Lake Linden which now houses the Heritage
Center.

L'Anse

Shrine of the Snowshoe Priest
Location: Lambert Rd. off US-41, 1 mile west of L'Anse, MI 49946.
Contact: (906) 353-6225, nhammer@up.net,
www.bishopbaraga.org/baragasites.htm. *Mail:* Bishop Baraga
Foundation, Inc., P.O. Box 665, Baraga, MI 49908. *Hours:* Open year-round, 24 hours a day. *Admission:* Donations accepted. *Site Info:* On-site
parking. Wheelchair accessible. Self-guided.
The enormity, location, and historic significance of the statue make it a
must-see for visitors. Rising six stories above the Red Rocks Bluff near
L'Anse, this historic shrine commands a breathtaking view of Michigan's
Keweenaw Bay. Holding a cross 7 ft. high and snowshoes 26 ft. long,
this handwrought brass sculpture of Bishop Baraga is 35 ft. tall, weighs
4 tons, and floats on a cloud of stainless steel supported by five
laminated wooden beams representing Bishop Baraga's five major
missions.

Mackinac Island

Mackinac Island State Park
Location: 7127 Huron Rd, Mackinac Island, MI.
Contact: (906) 847-3328, (231) 436-4100
mackinacparks@michigan.gov, www.mackinacparks.com. *Mail:* P.O.
Box 307, Mackinaw City, MI 49701. *Admission:* Various combination
tickets and family passes available, call or see website for details. *Site
Info:* Bike racks. Partially wheelchair accessible, see "Guide to
Accessibility" brochure at site. Self-guided with interpretive
demonstrations, call for group tours. *Events:* See website.

Originally established as a national park in 1875, over 80% of this automobile-free island is still park land containing natural wonders and many historic sites.

Fort Mackinac

Hours: May to mid-Oct 9am-4:30pm, Jul-Aug 9am-6pm. Constructed by the British during the American Revolution, Fort Mackinac served as an imposing sentinel in the Straits of Mackinac for 115 years. Inside the fort walls are 14 original buildings filled with interactive displays and period furnishings. Hear bugle music, rifle fire, and a cannon blast. Dance to a 19th-century tune, drill with soldiers, watch a court-martial reenactment, and play Victorian children's games.

Historic Downtown Mackinac

Hours: 11am-6pm, Mission Church 12-4pm.

From June 12-August 21, your Fort Mackinac ticket includes admission to 5 historic downtown Mackinac buildings. Several sites feature costumed historic interpreters and demonstrations. Buildings include: American Fur Company Store and Dr. Beaumont Museum (early 19th-century business & medical history), Biddle House (early 19th-century), Benjamin Blacksmith Shop (1950s era), McGulpin House, (late 18th-century, Michigan's oldest private residence), Mission Church (early 19th-century).

Richard and Jane Manoogian Mackinac Art Museum

Location: Indian Dormitory, Main St. Hours: Jul-Aug 10am-5:30pm, Aug-Oct 10am-4pm.

From Native American baskets to present-day paintings of the island by residents, this museum—located next to Marquette Park—showcases the historic art treasures in Mackinac State Historic Parks' collection.

Manistique

Schoolcraft County Historical Park

Location: Pioneer Park, Deer St., Manistique, MI 49854.
Contact: (906) 341-5045. *Mail:* P.O. Box 284. *Hours:* Jun-Labor Day Tue-Sat 12-4pm. *Admission:* Adults $1, Youth $0.50. *Site Info:* Free parking. Guides available. *Events:* Opening Day Festivities, Pioneer Days (Jun).

The Schoolcraft County Historical Society maintains this historical park containing the early 20th century Post House, an 1880s log cabin, and a restored 1922 water tower.

Marquette

Marquette Regional History Center

Location: 145 W. Spring St., Marquette, MI 49855.
Contact: (906) 226-3571, lammi@sbcglobal.net, www.marquettecohistory.org.
Mail: 213 N. Front St.
Hours: Mon-Fri 10am-5pm,
also Sat 11am-4pm in Jun-Aug. 2-year facility renovation underway, see website for updated hours & info. *Admission:* Adults $7, Students (13+) $3, Children 3 & under free. *Site Info:* On-site parking. ADA compliant accessibility. Self-guided, walking tour brochures available.
In 2010, the museum moved to a large facility across from the Marquette County Courthouse. Exhibit space includes 7,500 sq. ft. of state-of-the-art displays plus outdoor exhibits and depicts geologic and natural history, indigenous peoples, pioneer life, industry, and Yooper life. The 30,000 sq. ft. building includes a reception hall, education classroom, library, and museum store.

Menominee

Heritage Museum
Location: 904 11th Ave., Menominee, MI 49858.
Contact: (906) 863-9000, jcallow1@new.rr.com, krahgp@new.rr.com, dmurwin@new.rr.com, www.menomineehistoricalsociety.org
Mail: P.O. Box 151. *Hours:* Memorial Day to Labor Day Mon-Sat 10am-4pm. *Admission:* Donations accepted. *Site Info:* On-site parking. Wheelchair accessible. Group tours by appointment. *Events:* See website.
The Menominee County Historical Society tells the story of Menominee County's growth from 1863 using thousands of pictures, words, and artifacts. Located in the former St. John's Catholic Church, the museum exhibits highlight local history including native peoples, immigrants, industry, and a large miniature circus display.

Michigamme

Michigamme Museum
Location: 110 W. Main St., Michigamme, MI 49861.
Contact: (906) 323-6608, Michigammetownship@gmail.com.
Mail: P.O. Box 220. *Hours:* Memorial Day to Labor Day daily 12-5pm.
Admission: Donations accepted. *Site Info:* Street parking. Wheelchair accessible. Free guides available. *Events:* Log Cabin Day (Jun).
Exhibits include logging, mining, "Anatomy of a Murder," a log house, and a 1900 American LaFrance Steam Fire Engine.

Munising

Alger County Heritage Center
Location: 1496 Washington St., Munising, MI 49862.
Contact: (906) 387-4308, algerchs@jamadots.com. *Hours:* Tue-Sat 12-3pm. *Admission:* Free. *Site Info:* On-site parking. Wheelchair accessible.
Events: BBQ By the Bay (Jul), Alger Women's Roll of Honor (Aug), ACHS Annual Dinner.
The Heritage Center opened in 1993 in the former Washington Grade School. Exhibits feature historic Grand Island and the Grand Island Recreation Area, Munising Woodenware Company, barn building, homemaking, and the sauna. A fur trader's cabin and blacksmith shop are on site.

Negaunee

Michigan Iron Industry Museum
Location: 73 Forge Rd., Negaunee, MI 49866.
Contact: (906) 475-7857, friggenst@michigan.gov, www.michigan.gov/ironindustrymuseum. *Location:* US-41 East 1 mile west of M-35. *Hours:* May-Oct daily 9:30am-4:30pm, Apr 15-30 & Nov 1-15 Mon-Fri 9:30am-4pm. Call for winter hours. *Admission:* Free.
Site Info: On-site free parking. Wheelchair accessible. Self-guided.
Events: Iron, Steel, and the Automobile (Jun), Iron Ore and the Civil War (Aug), Weekday Lecture Series (Jul-Aug), Autumn Harvest Festival (Sep).
Overlooking the site of the first iron forge in the Lake Superior region, the museum interprets Michigan's rich mining heritage through exhibits, audio-visual programs, and outdoor interpretive paths. A large screen high-def film, "Iron Spirits: Life on the Michigan Iron Range," plays 7 times daily.

Newberry

Luce County Historical Museum
Location: 411 West Harrie St., Newberry, MI 49868.
Contact: (906) 293-3786, exploringthenorth.com/newberry/histmuseum.html, *Mail:* P.O. Box 41. *Hours:* Jun-Labor Day Tue-Thurs 2-4pm, also by appointment. *Admission:* Donations accepted.
Site Info: Free parking. Wheelchair accessible. Guides available.
Events: Open Houses (Jun & Sep).
The Luce County Historical Society was organized in 1975 to operate the former 1894 sheriff's residence and jail as a historical museum with displays of local artifacts and information. The 1894 brownstone, Queen Anne-style sheriff's residence with attached two-story jail contains the original kitchen, dining room, parlor, and bedrooms with related artifacts. Public areas contain jail cells, sheriff's office, and 1890 judge's bench with witness stand and jury chairs.

Tahquamenon Logging Museum

Location: North M-123, Newberry, MI 49868.
Contact: (906) 293-3700, www.superiorsights.com/logging museum/index.html. *Mail:* P.O. Box 254. *Hours:* Memorial Day to Labor Day daily 9am-5pm. *Admission:* Adults $3, Youth 6-12 $1.50, 5 & under free. *Site Info:* On-site parking. Wheelchair accessible. Guides available for a donation. *Events:* Lumberjack Breakfast (May-Aug), Music Festival & Breakfast (Jun-Aug), Breakfast & Logging Contests (During Newberry Oktoberfest).
The museum provides information about forestry and related activities. Features an authentic cook shack, original Civilian Conservation Corps building, CCC statue, DVD on CCC Camps, slide presentation on early logging in Michigan, logging truck, working sawmill, and a nature trail.

Ontonagon

Ontonagon Historical Museum

Location: 422 River St., Ontonagon, MI 49953.
Contact: (906) 884-6165, ochs@jamadots.com, www.ontonagon museum.org. *Hours:* Jan-May Mon-Fri 12-5pm, Jun-Dec Mon-Fri 10am-5pm & Sat 10am-4pm. *Admission:* Adults (16+) $3.
Site Info: Free on-site parking. Wheelchair accessible. Guide available by request. *Events:* Memorial Day and Labor Day weekend Open Houses, Monthly Dinner Programs by reservation.
This museum of the Ontonagon Historical Society portrays county history with emphasis on industry, lumber, and agriculture. The museum's collection includes rooms with period furniture, hundreds of antiques, and a collection of old newspapers and books.

Ontonagon Lighthouse

Hours: Lighthouse tours scheduled Jun to mid-Oct Sat-Sun 11am & 2pm and Mon-Fri 11am, 1pm, & 3pm. Off-season tours by appointment. *Admission:* Adults (18+) $5. *Site Info:* Park at museum, shuttle to lighthouse. Partially handicap accessible (1st floor only). Guided tours.
This simple, 1½ story, cream brick building from 1866 with a square light tower at the north end replaced an earlier wooden lighthouse. The light tower is three stories high, 39 ft. from the water to the focal plane. Decommissioned in 1964 and turned over to the Historical Society in 2003. Tours begin at the museum with the lighthouse's original 3rd order Fresnel lens.

Painesdale

Painesdale Mine and Shaft

Location: Shafthouse Rd., Painesdale, MI 49955.
Contact: (906) 482-0473, painesdalemineshaft@yahoo.com, www.painesdalemineshaft.com. *Mail:* P.O. Box 332. *Hours:* By appointment, call (906) 482-0473 or (906) 483-0031. *Admission:* Free.

Site Info: Free parking. Shafthouse and hoist building are wheelchair accessible. Guided tours only.

This volunteer group seeks to preserve and interpret the Champion #4 Shafthouse, built in 1902 and operated until 1967. Tours offered to the shafthouse, hoist house, and mining captain's office.

Pickford

Pickford Area Historical Society Museum
Location: 175 Main St., Pickford, MI 49774.
Contact: (906) 647-8851, kendi@lighthouse.net, www.pickfordareahistoricalsociety.org. *Mail:* P.O. Box 572.
Hours: Memorial Day to Labor Day Mon-Sat 10am-3pm, also by appointment (906) 297-3013. *Admission:* By donation. *Site Info:* Street parking. Wheelchair accessible. Self-guided. *Events:* Community Days, Golf Outing (Aug).

The society is restoring a brick 1915 former hardware building for a museum and cultural facility. Permanent exhibits and changing special displays feature early agricultural heritage, history of local churches, service organizations, clubs, and a large veteran's exhibit.

Rockland

Rockland Township Historical Museum
Location: 40 National Ave., Rockland, MI 49960.
Contact: (906) 886-2821, (906) 886-2645, rocklandmuseum@chartermi.net. *Mail:* P.O. Box 296. *Hours:* Memorial Day-Sep daily 11:30am- 4:30pm, also by appointment. *Admission:* Free.
Site Info: Free parking. Wheelchair accessible. Guides available.

The Rockland museum is dedicated to the history of the township's people, copper mines, businesses, and the first telephone system in the state of Michigan. Exhibits include historic home settings (kitchen, dining room, parlor, bedroom) and mining, faming, school, and military displays.

St. Ignace

Father Marquette National Memorial
Location: 720 Church St., Straits State Park, St. Ignace, MI 49781.
Contact: (906) 643-8620, burnettW@michigan.gov, www.michigan.gov/marquettememorial. *Hours:* Daily 8am-10pm.
Admission: Free. *Site Info:* State Parks Motor Vehicle Permit required for entry to park, not required to visit the memorial. Wheelchair accessible. Self-guided.

Part of the Michigan Historical Museum system, the memorial features hiking trails with historic interpretation and an open-air building dedicated to the memory of missionary and explorer Father Jacques Marquette. Views of the Mackinac Bridge.

Sault Ste. Marie

LeSault de Ste. Marie (Sault Historic Sites)
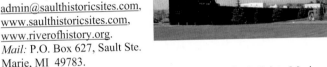
Contact: (906) 635-7082, admin@saulthistoricsites.com, www.saulthistoricsites.com, www.riverofhistory.org.
Mail: P.O. Box 627, Sault Ste. Marie, MI 49783.
Founded in 1967 to preserve, restore, and present Sault Sainte Marie history to visitors and local residents, the organization began with the acquisition of the Museum Ship Valley Camp and now offers several locations.

Museum Ship Valley Camp
Location: Corner of Johnson St. & Water St. *Contact:* (906) 632-3658. *Hours:* Mid-May to Jun daily 10am-5pm, Jul-Aug daily 9am-6pm, Sep-Oct daily 9:30am-5pm. *Admission:* Adults $11, Youth $5.50, combination tickets & group rates available. *Site Info:* On-site parking. Partially wheelchair accessible. Guide with tour.
This 550-foot bulk carrier was built in 1917, sailed until 1966, and was converted into a maritime museum in 1968. Visitors view all parts of the ship to see how a 29-person crew lived and worked. Cargo hold has displays of artifacts, paintings, shipwreck items, models and exhibits related to maritime history.

Tower of History
Location: 326 East Portage St. *Contact:* (906) 632-3658. *Hours:* Mid-May to mid-Oct daily 10am-5pm. *Admission:* Adults $6.50, Youth $3.25, combination tickets & group rates available. *Site Info:* Street or lot parking. Not wheelchair accessible. Guide with tour.
In addition to the story of the early missionaries, this 210-foot tower includes local and Native American history, exhibits, and a video presentation. The upper level features a 360-degree view of the Sault Locks and surrounding area.

River of History Museum
Location: 531 Ashmun St. *Contact:* (906) 632-1999. *Hours:* Mid-May to mid-Oct Mon-Sat 11am-5pm, closed major holidays. *Admission:* Adults $6.50, Youth $3.25. *Site Info:* Wheelchair accessible. Free audio wands available.
The 8,000-year history of St. Mary's River Valley, from glacial origins to Native American occupation, French fur trade, British expansion, and US Independence, is examined at the museum. The river tells her story of events witnessed, people met, and changes wrought along her shores and waters.

Water Street Historic Block
Contact: (906) 632-3658. *Admission:* By donation. *Site Info:* Street parking. Wheelchair accessible. Free guides available.

This cooperative effort between the Chippewa County Historical Society, Sault Historic Sites, and the City of Sault Ste. Marie includes the 1793 home of early fur trader John Johnston, the Henry Rowe Schoolcraft Office (the US's first Indian Agent), and the Kemp Industrial Museum (a museum of local industries in the former Kemp Coal Co. office).

Chippewa County Museum
Location: 115 Ashmun St., Sault Ste. Marie, MI 49783.
Contact: (906) 635-7082, cchs@sault.com. *Mail:* P.O. Box 342.
Hours: Call or email for schedule. Gift shop open seasonally Mon-Fri 1-4pm. *Admission:* Free. *Site Info:* On-site and street parking. Wheelchair access at back entrance. Self-guided. *Events:* "Dinner with the John Johnstons" dinner theater and "Celebrate with the Historic Churches of Sault Ste. Marie," Sault History Fest (Jul), live programming and craft demonstrations at the Johnston House (Jul-Aug).

This museum, maintained by the Chippewa County Historical Society, is located in an 1889 building that originally housed the Sault Ste. Marie News owned by Chase S. Osborn, the only governor to come from the Upper Peninsula. Inside are permanent and changing exhibits.

South Range

Copper Range Historical Museum
Location: 44 Trimountain Ave., South Range, MI 49963.
Contact: (906) 482-6125, johnandjeanp@chartermi.net, www.pasty.com/crhm.
Mail: P.O. Box 148.
Hours: Jun, Sep, & Oct Tue-Sat 12-3pm and Jul-Aug Mon-Sat

12-3pm. *Admission:* Adults $1 donation, Children & Members free.
Site Info: Free street parking. Not wheelchair accessible. Free group tours by appointment.

The museum, a Heritage Site of the Keweenaw National Historical Park, is located in the former South Range State Bank and seeks to create a sense of what life was like during the copper mining boom in the range towns of southern Houghton County. Displays include old mining clothes and tools, a logging display, and a general store display.

Vulcan

Iron Mountain Iron Mine
Location: US-2 (9 miles east of Iron Mountain), Vulcan, MI 49852.
Contact: (906) 563-8077, (906) 774-7914, ironmine@uplogon.com,
www.ironmountainironmine.com. *Mail:* P.O. Box 177, Iron Mountain,
MI 49801. *Hours:* Jun to mid-Oct 9am-5pm daily.
Admission: Adults $10, Children 6-12 $7.50, 5 & under free.
Site Info: Free parking. Guided tours.
The mine, operated from 1870-1945, produced over 22 million tons of
iron ore. Underground guided tours of the Iron Mine explain mining
operations.

Wakefield

Wakefield Museum
Location: 306 Sunday Lake St., Wakefield, MI 49968.
Contact: (906) 224-1045, djferson@baysat.net. *Mail:* P.O. Box 114.
Hours: Jun-Sep Tue-Sat 1-4pm. *Admission:* Donations accepted.
Site Info: Free parking. Self-guided. *Events:* "It's the Berries" (Jun),
"Fortchuly" Picnic (Jul), Christmas Fair (Dec).
Administered by the Wakefield Historical Society, the museum features
a classroom, general store, and mining exhibits.

Lower Peninsula

Acme

Music House Museum

Location: 7377 US-31 North, Acme, MI 49610.
Contact: (231) 938-9300, info@musichouse.org, www.musichouse.org. *Mail:* P.O. Box 297.
Hours: May-Oct Mon-Sat 10am-4pm, Sun 12pm-4pm. Nov-Dec Sat 10am-4pm. Daily Christmas-New Year's. *Admission:* Adults $10, Ages 6-15 $3, Family rate $25. *Site Info:* On-site parking. Wheelchair accessible. Guided tours. *Events:* Silent movie with Wurlitzer Theater Organ accompaniment. See website or call for event schedule.

Automatic music machines and instruments from the 1870s to the 1930s. Guided tours explain/demonstrate the unique instruments: Belgian dance organ, nickelodeons, music boxes, pipe organs, and the Wurlitzer Theater Organ. Collection includes a model of Traverse City circa 1930.

Ada

Averill Historical Museum

Location: 7144 Headley St., Ada, MI 49031.
Contact: (616) 676-9346, adahistoricalsociety@gmail.com, www.adahistoricalsociety.org. *Mail:* P.O. Box 741. *Hours:* Fri-Sun 1-4 pm, also by appointment. *Admission:* Donations accepted. *Site Info:* On-site and street parking. Wheelchair accessible. Self-guided or guided tours. *Events:* Arbor Day Celebration, Tri-Rivers Museum Tour (May), Arts in Ada (May), Music on the Lawn (Jun-Aug), August in Ada, Pioneer Summer Day Camp (Aug), Visit the Gardens (Aug), Pumpkin Carving Contest (Oct), Holiday Wreath Sale (Nov-Dec), Kids Cookie Decorating in the Barn (Dec).

Maintained by the Ada Historical Society, the museum features an exhibit on Rix Robinson, early trader on Grand River who came to Ada in 1821. Historic barn on property, historic farm gardens, oral history collection, and photo collection.

Adrian

Adrian Dominican Sisters
Motherhouse

Location: 1257 E. Siena Heights Dr.,
Adrian, MI 49221.
Contact: (517) 266-3580,
nfoley@adriandominicans.org,
www.adriandominicans.org. *Hours:* Mon-
Fri 9am-5pm, also by appointment.
Admission: Free. *Site Info:* Parking across
from Madden Hall. Wheelchair accessible.
Free guide available.
Adrian Dominican Sisters seek to discover
and identify themselves as women called
together to share faith and life with one
another. A display in Madden Hall, Adrian
Dominican Sisters: History and Mission, is organized in three time
periods: 1879-1933, 1933-1962, 1963-present. Each contains narrative
panels, photos, documents, and artifacts of the period.

Albion

Gardner House Museum
Location: 509 South Superior St. Albion, MI 49224.
Contact: (517) 629-5100, www.forks.org/history. *Hours:* Mother's Day to
Sep Sat-Sun 2-4pm. *Admission:* Donations accepted. *Site Info:* Free
parking. Guided tours available.
The 1875 home built by a local hardware merchant, Augustus P. Gardner,
was purchased by the Albion Historical Society in 1966. First floor rooms
reflect homes of 1875-1900. Second floor has WWII and 1920s displays.
Basement recreates workshop, 1900s kitchen, and country store. The
historical society's research collection located in Local History Room,
Albion Public Library, 501 S. Superior St.

Algonac

Algonac-Clay Museum
Location: 1240 St. Clair River Dr., Algonac, MI 48001.
Contact: (810) 794-7207, (810) 794-9015, achs@algonac-clay-
history.com, www.algonac-clay-history.com. *Mail:* P.O. Box 228.
Hours: Apr-Dec Sat-Sun 1-4pm, Jun-Aug Wed 7-9pm, also by
appointment. *Admission:* Free. *Site Info:* On-site parking. Wheelchair
accessible. Free audio and live guides available. *Events:* Log Cabin Day
(Jun), Spaghetti Dinner fundraiser (Oct).
Volunteers of the Algonac-Clay Historical Society staff the museum in
the Bostwick building, former doctor's office, township hall, and library.
With one of the longest deep water ports in Michigan, the area is known

as a hospitality port on the Great Lakes for Tallships. The society also operates a log cabin in Clay Township. Displays include Chris-Craft, Gar Wood, Harsens Island, and the shipping industry.

Allegan

Old Jail Museum
Location: 113 Walnut St., Allegan, MI 49010.
Contact: (269) 673-8292, oldjailmuseum06@yahoo.com, www.allegancountyhistoricalmuseum.org. *Hours:* Fri-Sat 10am-4pm, also by appointment. *Admission:* Donations accepted. *Site Info:* Street parking. Not wheelchair accessible. Guided tours, advance notice required for large groups. *Events:* Historic Village at the Fair includes over 15 historic structures, open during Fiber Fest (Aug) and Allegan County Fair (Sep). The Allegan County Historical Society acquired the old jail in 1963 and converted it to a museum with period rooms and displays. The Society also maintains John C. Pahl Historic Village at the Allegan Fair Grounds. Accredited by the American Association of Museums and listed in the National Register of Historic Places. Exhibits from Pioneer Days to 1950. Their collection includes artifacts from the War of 1812, the Civil War, the Spanish-American War, WWI, and WWII.

Alto

Bowne Township Historical Museum
Location: 8240 Alden Nash Ave., Alto, MI 49302.
Contact: (616) 868-6846, srjohnson4@charter.net, www.bownehistory.org.
Mail: P.O. Box 35. *Hours:* Jun-Sep, 1st Sun of month 2-4pm.
Admission: Free. *Site Info:* Free parking. Museum is partially

wheelchair accessible, schoolhouse is not. Self-guided. *Events:* Spring Grand Opening May 1-2 11am-5pm in conjunction with Tri-River Museum Network.
This two-story museum building administered by the Bowne Township Historical Society contains memorabilia, artifacts, genealogy information, and historical items. Bowne Center Schoolhouse (SE corner of 84th and Alden Nash Ave.) is a turn-of-century structure on the National One Room School Registry. It contains historical information about eight one-room schools in the township and is filled with old-fashioned desks, a collection of old schoolbooks, and other school items.

Cascade Museum
Location: 2839 Thornapple River Dr., Alto, MI 49302.
Contact: (616) 868-6465, morningspirit@comcast.net. *Mail:* 5588 Buttrick SE. *Hours:* By appointment. *Admission:* Free. *Site Info:* Public

parking. Wheelchair accessible. Guides available by appointment.
Events: Christmas Tree Lighting.
A museum of Cascade local history is maintained by the Cascade
Historical Society in the 1890 township hall.

Ann Arbor

Bentley Historical Library
Location: University of Michigan,
1150 Beal Ave., Ann Arbor, MI
48109.
Contact: (734) 764-3482,
bentley.ref@umich.edu,
www.bentley.umich.edu.
Hours: Mon-Fri 9am-5pm.

Admission: Free. *Site Info:* Free on-site parking. Wheelchair accessible.
Established in 1935 by the Regents of the University of Michigan, the
library moved to its current building in 1972 and is comprised of three
divisions: the Michigan Historical Collections, the University Archives
and Records Program, and Access and Reference Services. The library
has amassed extensive holdings on the history of the state and of the
university which are consulted by Michigan's citizens and others from
across the nation and around the world.

Gerald R. Ford Presidential Library
Location: 1000 Beal Ave., Ann Arbor, MI 48109.
Contact: (734) 205-0555, ford.library@nara.gov,
www.fordlibrarymuseum.gov. *Hours:* Mon-Fri 8:30am-5pm, closed on
federal holidays.
The Library (archives), together with the Gerald R. Ford Presidential
Museum in Grand Rapids, comprises a unit of the National Archives and
Records Administration system of presidential libraries. The Library's
collection includes 20 million pages of letters, memos, meeting notes,
plans, reports and oral histories, plus audiovisual materials from the
congressional, vice presidential, and presidential papers of Gerald Ford
and his White House staff. Also included are personal papers of persons
active in national politics and the Federal government, especially in the
1960s and 1970s, and selected federal agency records from that period.

Kempf House Museum
Location: 312 S. Division St., Ann Arbor, MI 48104.
Contact: (734) 994-4898, kempfhousemuseum@gmail.com,
www.kempfhousemuseum.org. *Hours:* Sun 1-4pm, also by appointment.
Admission: Donations accepted. *Site Info:* Nearby parking. Wheelchair
accessible. Guides available. *Events:* German Christmas Open House
(Dec), Valentine Teas (Feb). Noon lectures featuring topics of historical
interest and special events throughout the year.
A modest temple-style Greek Revival house built in 1853 is maintained
by the Ann Arbor Department of Parks and Recreation and administered
by a volunteer board of directors. Listed in the National Register of
Historic Places. Tour guides tell the story Reuben and Pauline Kempf,

prominent German-American musicians who taught piano and voice lessons in the house for over 60 years. Victorian furnishings include the Kempf's historic 1877 Steinway grand piano.

Museum on Main Street

Location: 500 N. Main at Beakes St., Ann Arbor, MI 48106.
Contact: (734) 662-9092, wchs-500@ameritech.net, www.washtenawhistory.org.
Mail: P.O. Box 3336.
Hours: Wed, Sat-Sun 12-4pm, also by appointment.
Admission: Free. *Events:* Six special programs per year,

antique appraisals every other year. Call or see website for information. The Washtenaw County Historical Society society fosters interest in the history of the county from the time of the original inhabitants to the present through the preservation and presentation of artifacts and information by exhibit, assembly, and publication. Exhibits change quarterly. Collection includes over 5,000 artifacts, most county-related, gathered over 160 years.

Southerland-Wilson Farm Museum

Location: 797 Textile Rd., Ann Arbor, MI 48106.
Contact: (734) 971-2384, donbet@comcast.net, salvette@umich.edu, www.pittsfieldhistory.org. *Mail:* P.O. Box 6013. *Hours:* By appointment only.
The Pittsfield Township Historical Society maintains displays at the Pittsfield Community Center and Township Administration Building (6201 W. Michigan Ave.) and is restoring the township-owned Sutherland-Wilson farmhouse. The farm, settled by Lanford Sutherland in 1832, stayed in the family until 2000 and is listed in the National Register of Historic Places.

William L. Clements Library

Location: 909 S. University Ave., University of Michigan, Ann Arbor, MI 48109.
Contact: (734) 764-2347, clements.library@umich.edu, www.clements.umich.edu. *Hours:* Exhibit Area Labor Day to Memorial Day Mon-Fri 1-4:45pm, Memorial Day to Labor Day Mon-Thurs 9am-5:45pm, Fri 9-11:45am. Closed university holidays. *Admission:* Free.
Site Info: Metered street parking. Wheelchair accessible. Self-guided.
This major academic reserach library collects and preserves primary source materials and creates an environment that supports and encourages scholarly investigation of our nation's past. Public functions are restricted to changing exhibits in the front hall focusing on aspects of the collections that would interest both an expert bibliophile and the casual reader.

Arcadia

Arcadia Area Historical Museum
Location: 3340 Lake St., Arcadia, MI 49613.
Contact: (231) 889-3389, ej.howard@yahoo.com, www.arcadiami.com.
Mail: P.O. Box 67. *Hours:* Jun Thurs-Sat 1-4pm, Sun 1-3pm. Also by
appointment. *Admission:* Free. *Site Info:* On-site parking. Wheelchair
accessible. Self-guided. *Events:* Cracker Barrel Sessions.
The Arcadia Area Historical Society manages this township museum in an
1884 Victorian house built by early settler Howard Gilbert. Exhibits tell
the story of the Arcadia Furniture Company, the Arcadia & Betsey River
Railway, shipping and logging in early community history, the Arcadia
Channel, the sunken Minnehaha, area baseball, the local United Methodist
Church, Historic Trinity Lutheran Church, and Harriet Quimby: America's
first Lady in the Air.

Atlanta

McKenzie One-Room School
Location: M-33 N. (Montmorency Fair Grounds), Atlanta, MI.
Contact: (989) 742-4218. *Mail:* P.O. Box 252, Hillman, MI 49746.
Hours: 3rd week in Aug 10am-9pm. *Admission:* Fair entry fee.
Site Info: Fairground parking. Wheelchair accessible. Live presentations.
The Montmorency County Historical Society maintains the school on the
Montmorency County fairgrounds. Artifacts are stored within the
building; antiques are exhibited and judged during Fair Week.

Barryton

Barryton Museum
Location: 19730 30th Ave., Barryton, MI 49305.
Contact: (989) 382-7334, (989) 382-5419, ikgibbons@hughes.net.
Hours: Memorial Day to Labor Day Sat-Sun 1-4pm. *Events:* Barryton
Lilac Fest (May), Christmas tree lighting (Dec).
In addition to the museum, which opened 1987, the Barryton Area
Historical Commission also maintains Titus School, Covert School, and
Ed McNeilly Memorial Building.

Battle Creek

Heritage Battle Creek
Location: 165 N. Washington, Battle Creek, MI 49017.
Contact: (269) 965-2613, bcarch@net-link.net,
www.heritagebattlecreek.org. *Hours:* Office Mon-Fri 9am-5pm.
Admission: Free. *Site Info:* Free parking. Partially wheelchair accessible.
Self-guided, guided tours of Kimball House available Sun or by

appointment. *Events:* Strawberry Festival and Ice Cream Social (Jun), Child's Christmas Past Victorian Christmas (Dec).

Formed in 1999 as administrative agency for the Historical Society of Battle Creek and Sojourner Truth Institute, HBC maintains collections and operates the Kimball House Museum. Provides two heritage tours. "Freedom Saga" tells the story of Sojourner Truth and the underground railroad in southwest Michigan, "Road to Wellness" traces Seventh-Day Adventist origins of health reform and the development of the cereal industry.

Historic Adventist Village

Location: 411 Champion St., Battle Creek, MI 49017.
Contact: (269) 965-3000, adventistvillage@tds.net, www.adventistheritage.org. *Hours:* Memorial Day to Labor Day Sun-Fri 10am-5pm, Sat 2-5pm. *Admission:* By donation. *Site Info:* Free parking at 480 W. Van Buren St. Wheelchair accessible. Guided tour available. This recreated 19th century village takes visitors back in time with reenactments and restored and replicated buildings. Visitors view living history in a log cabin, one-room schoolhouse, and other houses and churches of the Adventist pioneers who settled in Battle Creek over 150 years ago. The Dr. J.H. Kellogg Discovery Center located in the village offers a fun learning experience for all ages. Visitors learn about health treatments and practices of more than a century ago while discovering health principles that put Battle Creek on the map as the Cereal Capital of the World.

Bay City

Historical Museum of Bay County

Location: 321 Washington Ave, Bay City, MI 48708.
Contact: (989) 893-5733, rbloomfield@bchsmuseum.org, www.bchsmuseum.org.
Hours: Mon-Fri 10am-5pm, Sat 12-4pm. Archives: Tue-Thurs

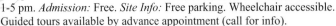

1-5 pm. *Admission:* Free. *Site Info:* Free parking. Wheelchair accessible. Guided tours available by advance appointment (call for info).
Events: River of Time (Sep), Tour of Homes (Oct).

Bay County Historical Society's museum in a former armory features the DeMara Gallery, a collection of period rooms, the story of Bay City's maritime history told in the Kantzler Maritime Gallery, and its newest gallery: "Bay County... Trails Through Time," a 3,700-square-foot gallery featuring the distinctive heritage of Bay County from pre-contact days to present.

Beaver Island

Beaver Island Heritage Park
Location: 26275 Main St., Beaver Island, MI 49782.
Contact: (231) 448-2254, history@beaverisland.net,
www.beaverisland.net/History. *Mail:* P.O. Box 263. *Hours:* Jun to Labor
Day Mon-Sat 11am-5pm, Sun 12-3pm. *Admission:* Donations accepted.
Site Info: Free parking. Guides available. *Events:* Museum Week (Jul).
The Heritage Park includes the Old Mormon Print Shop Museum, the
printing operation for James Strang's Kingdom of St. James, 1850-1856,
now the general history museum for Beaver Island. The Beaver Island
Maritime Museum was a net house built in 1906 and restored in 1980 to
display fishing and shipping history of the island. The Protar Home, the
log cabin of Feodar Protar, is undergoing restoration. The Francis E.
Martin Commercial Fishing Museum will feature 50-ft. wooden gill net
tug, the Bob S.

Belding

Belding Museum
Location: 108 Hanover St., Belding, MI 48809.
Contact: (616) 794-1900, kthomas@ci.belding.mi.us,
www.ci.belding.mi.us/pages/community/museum.html. *Mail:* P.O. Box
45. *Hours:* 1st Sun of month 1-4pm. *Admission:* Free. *Site Info:* On-site
parking. Wheelchair accessible. Guided tours by appointment.
Events: Tri-Rivers "Spring Into the Past" weekend (May), Labor Day
Open House, quilt show, Breakfast with Santa.
The Museum in the 1906 Belrockton Dormitory, for single women
working at Belding Brothers and Co. Silk Mill, is administered by a 7-
member board appointed by the Belding City Council. The board collects,
preserves, and presents the natural, cultural, and social history of Belding
area. The collection's focus is on the silk mill industry era of 1880-1935.

Bellaire

Bellaire Historical Museum
Location: 202 N. Bridge St.,
Bellaire, MI 49615.
Contact: (231) 533-8631,
wallays1@aol.com. *Mail:* P.O.
Box 646. *Hours:* Tue-Sat 11am-
3pm. *Admission:* Free.
Site Info: Street parking.
Wheelchair accessible. Guide
available.

Formed in 1975, the Bellaire Area Historical Society has worked to
maintain the area's artifacts, social history, and copies of newspapers from
1885 to current issues. Exhibits include products produced at the local
woodenware factory beginning in 1879.

Belleville

Belleville Area Museum
Location: 405 Main St., Belleville, MI 48111.
Contact: (734) 697-1944, dwilson@provide.net, www.vanburen-mi.org/Museum/Belleville_Area_Museum.html. *Hours:* Winter Tue-Sat 12-4pm, May to Labor Day Mon-Fri 12-4pm. *Admission:* Adults $1, Ages 6-17 $.50, Families $3, Tours $1/person. *Site Info:* On-site parking. Wheelchair accessible. Self-guided. *Events:* Quilt exhibit (Mar), Festival of Holiday Trees (Dec).
The Belleville Area Historical Society maintains this museum in the 1875 Van Buren Township Hall, hosting exhibits highlighting the local history of Van Buren and Sumpter Townships and the city of Belleville.

Bellevue

Bellevue Museum
Location: 212 N. Main St., Bellevue, MI 49021.
Contact: (616) 763-9049, bellevue_mi@cox.net, www.rootsweb.com/~mibhs/. *Hours:* Wed 2-4pm, also by appointment. *Admission:* Free. *Site Info:* Street parking. Wheelchair accessible. Free guided tour available by appointment.
The museum is located in the same building as the local library. Exhibits feature items pertaining to local history.

Benton Harbor

Mary's City of David
Location: 1158 E. Britain Ave., Benton Harbor, MI 49023.
Contact: (269) 925-1601, rjtaylor@maryscityofdavid.org, www.maryscityofdavid.org. *Mail:* P.O. Box 187. *Hours:* Jun-Sep Sat-Sun 1-5 pm, also by appointment. *Admission:* Museum admission $1, tours $4. *Site Info:* Free parking. Partially wheelchair accessible. Guided tours beginning 1:30 pm at museum. *Events:* See website.
The Israelite House of David was founded in 1902 in Fostoria, OH, and moved to Benton Harbor in 1903 where it reorganized in 1930 under the surviving cofounder, Mary Purnell. The sect's roots go back to the Philadelphian Society in England in 1652. Tours include the print shop, carpenter shop, powerhouse, greenhouse, Shiloh Gardens, Synagogue, and Eastman Springs.

Berrien Springs

History Center at Courthouse Square
Location: 313 N. Cass St., Berrien Springs, MI 49103.
Contact: (269) 471-1202, fporter@berrienhistory.org,
www.berrienhistory.org. *Mail:* P.O. Box 261. *Hours:* Sep-May Mon-Fri
10am-5pm, Jun-Aug Mon-Sat 10am-5pm. *Admission:* Free.
Site Info: Free on-site parking. Partially wheelchair accessible. Guided
tours available by appointment. *Events:* Motor Coach Tour, Pioneer Day,
Summer Program Series, Holiday Open House.
Operated by the Berrien County Historical Association, the History
Center includes Michigan's oldest complex of county government
buildings: the 1839 Courthouse, 1830 Log House, 1870 Sheriff's
Residence, 1820/1873 Office Building, and Blacksmith's Shop. The
BCHA publishes books and offers programs relevant to the history of the
area. The museum features permanent and special exhibits highlighting
regional history.

Big Rapids

Jim Crow Museum of Racist Memorabilia
Location: 820 Campus Dr., Ferris State Univ., Big Rapids, MI 49307.
Contact: (231) 591-5873, jimcrowmuseum@ferris.edu,
www.ferris.edu/jimcrow. *Hours:* Mon-Fri 8am-5pm by appointment.
Admission: Free.
The museum fosters racial understanding and healing through promoting
scholarly examination of historical and contemporary expressions of
racism. It serves as an educational and research resource for university
courses and human rights organizations and collects, exhibits, and
preserves objects and collections related to racial segregation, civil rights,
and racial caricatures.

Mecosta County Historical Society Museum
Location: 129 S. Stewart Ave., Big Rapids, MI 49307.
Contact: (231) 592-5091, verona705@chartermi.net. *Hours:* Sat 2-4pm,
also by appointment. *Admission:* Free. *Site Info:* Street parking or County
Court parking lot. Not wheelchair accessible. Free guide available.
Events: Victorian Tea with hat show and vintage cars.
The society, organized in 1894, operates the present museum opened in
1966 in the former home of lumberman Fitch Phelps. Exhibits include
historical displays about the Mecosta County area and the lumber
industry.

Birmingham

Birmingham Historical Museum and Park
Location: 556 W. Maple, Birmingham, MI 48009.
Contact: (248) 530-1928, museum@ci.birmingham.mi.us,
www.bhamgov.org/museum. *Hours:* Wed-Sat 1-4 pm, also by
appointment. *Admission:* Adults $2, Seniors/Students $1, under 5 free

(includes tours of the Allen and Hunter houses). *Site Info:* 2 hours free parking at Chester Street parking structure. Wheelchair accessible. Guided tours available. *Events:* Little Christmas Tea, Memorial Day Open House, Birmingham Hay Day (Fall), Pioneer Tour of Greenwood Cemetery, New Year's Eve Family Fun Night.
The Museum, founded in 2001, maintains collections focusing on Birmingham/Bloomfield Twp. area history. Two historic buildings, the 1822 John West Hunter House and the 1928 Allen House, reside in a historical park. Their collection includes Michigan pioneering artifacts c. 1820-1880, a local history collection, and a period costume collection c. 1840-1960.

Breckenridge

Plank Road and Drake House Memorial Museums
Location: 382 and 404 E. Saginaw St., Breckenridge, MI 48615. *Contact:* (517) 842-1241, dandlbriggs@peoplepc.com. *Mail:* P.O. Box 52. *Hours:* May-Oct: Mon 9am-12pm. *Admission:* Free. *Site Info:* Limited parking. Wheelchair accessible. *Events:* Heritage Day Music Fest (Aug).
The Breckenridge-Wheeler Area Historical Society maintains two museum buildings: the Plank Road Museum in the 1890 Baptist Church and the Drake House Memorial Museum. Exhibits examine local farming, businesses, music, lumbering, and a period 1910 doctor's home.

Brethren

Brethren Heritage Museum

Location: corner of Cart and Amick, Brethren, MI 49619. *Contact:* (231) 477-5526, janetdonstroup@yahoo.com, www.allartsmanistee.com. *Mail:* 17955 Coates Hwy. *Hours:* Jun-Sep Sun 1-4pm.
Admission: Donations accepted. *Site Info:* Free parking. Wheelchair accessible. Guides available by appointment at (231) 477-5525 or (231) 477-5539. *Events:* Biennial 5th Grade "Walk through Time," Labor Day "Heritage Lane," Fall Fun Fest (Oct). Check website info.
The museum, located in a former store and ice house, hosts exhibits on logging, township schools, and the Pere Marquette railroad "High Bridge."

Bridgeport

Bridgeport Historic Village and Museum
Location: 6190 Dixie Hwy., Bridgeport, MI 48722.
Contact: (989) 777-5230, bridgeporthistorical@gmail.com,
www.bridgeporthistorical.blogspot.com. *Mail:* P.O. Box 561.
Hours: Tue-Sat 1-5 pm, also by appointment. Special tours or children's
historic school day ($6/child) by reservation. *Admission:* Free.
Site Info: Nearby parking. Wheelchair accessible. Guides available upon
request. *Events:* School Childrens' Pioneer Days (May), Pioneer
Christmas (Dec), Flea Market at Bridgeport Days, Concerts in the Park,
Movies in the Park.
The museum, opened in 1972, is administered by the Historical Society of
Bridgeport. Exhibits include a 1912 Ford Model T touring car and an
antique fire truck. The Historic Village features public gardens, a
childrens' garden, and restored buildings including a barn, one-room
schoolhouse, 1854 Hannay House, 1896 Bridgeport Township Hall,
gazebo, replica fire house, and a veterans' memorial.

Brighton

Lyon Schoolhouse Memorial Museum
Location: 1145 Bund Rd., Brighton, MI 48116.
Contact: (810) 250-7276, info@brightonhistorical.com,
www.brightonareahistorical.com. *Mail:* P.O. Box 481. *Hours:* Thurs 9am-
4pm, 3rd Sun of month 1-4pm. *Admission:* free. *Site Info:* On-site
parking. Wheelchair accessible.
The museum, administered by the Brighton Area Historical Society, is
located in an 1855 frame construction, one-room schoolhouse. The school
has been refurbished for visitors to experience the one-room setting of a c.
1900 rural American school. Special class programs for schoolchildren in
fall and spring allow a day-long immersion in the period. Museum
displays examine tools used in rural life and early veterinary tools from
local vet Dr. George Schaeffer.

Cobach Center
Location: 202 W. Main St.
Contact: (810) 229-2784. *Hours:* Tue-Sun 5-8pm, Sat also 9am-
12pm. *Admission:* Free. *Site Info:* Street parking. Not wheelchair
accessible.
Located in the 1879, two-story brick building that once housed the
local fire department and city hall, the Cobach Center hosts historical
displays, reenactments, theatrical performances, and art exhibits. The
City of Brighton Arts, Culture, and History Center is located next to
the millpond and adjacent to the 1837 Brighton Old Village
Cemetery. Cemetery open daily, information available at the Cobach
Center.

Brooklyn

Walker Tavern
Historic Complex
Location: 13220 M-50,
Brooklyn, MI 49230.
Contact: (517) 467-4401,
www.michigan.gov/walker
tavern, *Hours:* Memorial
Day to Labor Day Wed-
Sun 9:30am-4:30pm.

Admission: Free. *Site Info:* Free parking. Partially wheelchair accessible.
Events: Walker on Wheels, Frontier Fest, Farmers Market.
This 19th century stagecoach stop on the road between Detroit and
Chicago was operated by Sylvester Walker at Cambridge Junction. The
tavern includes an 1840s parlor, barroom, dining room, and kitchen. The
barn offers surveying and stagecoach exhibits. Part of the Michigan
Historical Museum System.

Byron Center

Byron Center Historical Museum
Location: 2506 Prescott SW., Byron Center, MI 49315.
Contact: (616) 878-0888, byronmuseum@sbcglobal.net,
www.byroncenterhistory.com. *Mail:* P.O. Box 20. *Hours:* Mon & Wed
12-3pm, Tue & Thurs 10am-4pm, Last Sat of month 12-3pm.
Admission: Free. *Site Info:* On-site parking. Wheelchair accessible. Guide
available. *Events:* Byron Days (Jul), Annual Old Homes Tour (Sep).
Formed in 1978 to do genealogical research, the Byron Center Historical
Society secured the historic Township Hall in 1986 for a museum.
Displays feature an exploration of a variety of locations: lumber, post
office, doctor's office, one-room school, church, and a period home.

Cadillac

Wexford County Historical Society
Location: 127 Beech St. Cadillac, MI 49601.
Contact: (231) 779-0767. *Mail:* P.O. Box 124. *Hours:* Memorial Day to
Labor Day Wed-Sat 12-4pm. *Admission:* Free.
Located in the former Cadillac Carnegie Library, the Society presents the
history of Wexford County through displays, photos, and printed material.

Caledonia

Caledonia Historical Museum
Location: Caledonia Library, 240 Emmons, Caledonia, MI 49316.
Contact: (616) 647-3840. *Hours:* Call current hours. *Admission:* Free.

The museum collection, maintained by the Caledonia Historical Society in the History Room of the Caledonia Township Branch Library, includes artifacts, local history, and genealogical resources.

Cannonsburg

Cannon Township Historical Museum
Location: 8045 Cannonsburg Rd., Cannonsburg, MI 49317.
Contact: (616) 874-6865. *Mail:* P.O. Box 24. *Hours:* May-Sep Sun 2-4pm, also by appointment. *Admission:* Free. *Site Info:* Nearby parking. Wheelchair accessible. Self-guided.
The Cannon Township Historical Society preserves township history in the former township hall. Collection includes school and family photographs, machinery, furniture, household goods, and the local genealogy collection.

Canton

Canton Historical Society
Location: 2020 Canton Center Rd., Canton, MI 48187.
Contact: (734) 397-0088, lizcarlson@comcast.net. *Mail:* P.O. Box 87362. *Hours:* Tue 1-4pm, Thurs 2-5pm, Sat 10am-4pm, also by appointment. *Admission:* Free. *Site Info:* Nearby parking. Wheelchair accessible. Guides available.

An original one-room school contains exhibits highlighting agricultural, military, and social history plus an agricultural exhibition in the barn and tours of the historic Bartlett-Travis house. The society's research library is located onsite.

Capac

Capac Community Museum and Kempf Historical Center
Location: 401 E. Kempf Ct., Capac, MI 48014.
Contact: (810) 395-2859. *Mail:* P.O. Box 64. *Hours:* May-Oct Sun 1-4pm, Mon-Sat by apointment. *Admission:* Donations accepted.
Site Info: On-site parking. Wheelchair accessible. Guides available.
Events: Memorial Day Summer Kick-Off, Quilt Show (Jul), Fall Dinner (Oct).
The Museum, located in the restored Grand Trunk Depot, and the Kempf Historical Center host exhibits including the Kempf Model City (a mechanical city, 40 feet long and 4 feet wide), a milk bottle collection with over 500 milk bottles from towns in the Thumb of Michigan, a Fairbanks-Morris Speeder Car, and a 1903 wood-rimmed bicycle.

Caseville

Caseville Historical Museum
Location: Maccabees Hall, 6733 Prospect St., Caseville, MI 48725.
Contact: (989) 856-9090, chscm@comcast.net,
www.thehchs.org/caseville. *Mail:* P.O. Box 1973. *Hours:* Wed-Thurs-Sat
11:30am-4:30pm, daily. *Admission:* Free. *Site Info:* On-site parking.
Wheelchair accessible. Docent available. *Events:* Ice cream social
(Memorial Day weekend).
The Historical Society of Caseville maintains a museum in the 1880s
Maccabees Hall featuring displays of local history.

Cassopolis

Brick School
Location: 63600 Brick Church St., Cassopolis, MI 49031.
Contact: (269) 454-2907. *Hours:* By appointment. *Site Info:* On-site
parking.
The Cass County Historical Commission invites you to step back in time
to experience education in a one-room rural school with old books,
furniture, and maps.

Central Lake

Knowles Historical Museum
Location: 2238 S. Main, M-88., Central Lake, MI 49622.
Contact: lois@torchlake.com. *Mail:* P.O. Box 404. *Hours:* Wed-Fri 1-
4pm, also by appointment. *Admission:* Free. *Site Info:* Street parking. Not
wheelchair accessible.
The Central Lake Area Historical Society documents and preserves area
history for future generations by collecting and presenting local historical
items in the museum. This restored home is furnished with local period
furniture.

Centreville

Centreville Museum and Historic Library
Location: 113 E. Main St., Centreville, MI 49032-5141.
Contact: (269) 503-0196, mstarmann@yahoo.com. *Mail:* P.O. Box 492. *Hours:* Mon, Fri-Sat 10am-5pm. *Admission:* Free. *Site Info:* On-site
parking. Not wheelchair accessible. Self-guided.
This museum operated by the St. Joseph County Historical Society is
located in the historic 1863 Old Klesner Hotel.

Charlevoix

Harsha House Museum

Location: 103 State St., Charlevoix, MI 49720.
Contact: (231) 547-0373, chxhistory@sbcglobal.net,
www.chxhistory.com. *Mail:* P.O. Box 525. *Hours:* Mar-Apr Thurs-Sat 1-4pm, May-Jun & Sep-Dec Tue-Sat 1-4pm, Jul-Aug Mon-Sat 1-4pm.
Admission: $1 suggested donation. *Site Info:* Free street and lot parking.
Wheelchair accessible. Free guides available. *Events:* See website.
The Charlevoix Historical Society maintains the museum in the 1891
Queen Anne home of early businessman Horace Harsha. Museum
includes 3 period rooms, local history artifacts, rotating exhibits, the Bob
Miles collection of 15,000 photographs, original artwork, Hemingway's
original marriage license, and a research library. The 1892 Railroad Depot
at the end of Chicago Avenue on Depot Beach is also administered by the
Society.

Charlotte

Eaton County's Museum at Courthouse Square

Location: 100 W. Lawrence Ave.
Charlotte, MI 48813.
Contact: (517) 543-6999, preserve@ia4u.net,
www.visitcourthousesquare.org. *Mail:* P.O.
Box 411, *Hours:* Mon-Fri 9am-4pm.
Admission: $3 Adults (12 & older),
Wednesday is free day. *Site Info:* Free street
and lot parking. Partially wheelchair
accessible, call for details. Free guide
available, call for school group admission
rates. *Events:* Celebrate Charlotte, Frontier
Days, wine and beer tastings, formal
Christmas dinner.
Maintained by the Courthouse Square Association the 1885 Courthouse,
1845 Courthouse, and the 1873 Sheriff Residence, home of the Chamber
of Commerce. Permanent exhibits focus on the history of the buildings
and of the county.

Cheboygan

Cheboygan County Historical Museum

Location: 427 Court St., Cheboygan, MI 49721.
Contact: (616) 627-9597, cheboyganmuseum@gmail.com. *Mail:* P.O.
Box 5005. *Hours:* June-Labor Day Tue-Sat 1-4pm. *Admission:* Adults $5,
children free. *Site Info:* Free parking. Self-guided. *Events:* Autumnfest,
Festival of Trees.
The Historical Society of Cheboygan County maintains a museum and a

schoolhouse with replica 1880s desks, a dunce cap, and a stool. The museum's displays examine the history of the Cheboygan area and change annually in Fall.

Chesaning

Chesaning Historical Museum
Location: 602 W. Broad St., Chesaning, MI 48616.
Contact: (989) 845-3155, cahs@centurytel.net, www.cahs.chesaning.com.
Mail: P.O. Box 52. *Hours:* 1st Sat each month, Apr-Nov 1-4pm. Also by appointment. *Admission:* Free. *Site Info:* Wheelchair accessible.
Located in the former St. John's Episcopal Church, the museum is run by the Chesaning Area Historical Society. Changing displays and permanent exhibits focus on area history within the Chesaning Union School District from Indian habitation to present. Exhibits include local industries, Farmer Peet, Roycraft mobile homes, the Chesaning Showboat, and one-room schools.

Chesterfield

Chesterfield Museum and Historic Village
Location: 47275 Sugarbush Rd., Chesterfield, MI 48047.
Contact: (586) 949-3810, (586) 749-3713, chesterfieldhistory@yahoo.com, www.chesterfieldhistoricalsociety.org.
Hours: Jun-Aug 2nd Sun of month 1-3pm. *Admission:* Free.
Site Info: Limited on-site parking. Wheelchair accessible. Free private tours available. *Events:* Log Cabin Day (Jun), Township Tree Lighting (Dec). Open House (Sep) offers an opportunity to see all the buildings, working blacksmith shop, and a classic car display with games, activities, and children's craft demonstrations.
The Chesterfield Township Historical Society, founded in 1993 to preserve the history of Chesterfield Township, opened the Historic Village in 2006 containing the 1862 Weller School, a log cabin, a cobbler shop, and a blacksmith shop.

Clarkston

Clarkston Heritage Museum
Location: 6495 Clarkston Rd., Clarkston, MI 48346.
Contact: (248) 922-0270, info@clarkstonhistorical.org, www.clarkstonhistorical.org, *Hours:* Mon-Thurs 10am-9pm, Fri 10am-6pm, Sat 10am-5pm, Sun 1-5pm (closed Sun in summer).
Admission: Free. *Site Info:* On-site parking. Wheelchair accessible. Self-guided. *Events:* Art in the Village juried art show (Sep).
The 250-member Clarkston Community Historical Society is dedicated to preserving local history through family programs, lectures, and publications. Rotating exhibits are hosted in the museum.

Clinton Township

Clinton Township Historical Village
Location: 40700 Romeo Plank Rd., Clinton Township, MI 48038.
Contact: (586) 263-9173, jphungerford@gmail.com, www.ctwphc.org. *Hours:* Call or check website for hours.
Admission: Free. *Site Info:* Free

parking. Wheelchair accessible. Guides available.
The Township Historical Commission is responsible for the general administration of historical properties including buildings in the Clinton Township Historical Village. The interpretive program is operated jointly with the Greater Clinton Township Historical Society.

Coloma

North Berrien Historical Museum
Location: 300 Coloma Ave., Coloma, MI 49038.
Contact: (269) 468-3330, nbhsmuseum@sbcglobal.net, www.northberrienhistory.org. *Mail:* P.O. Box 207. *Hours:* May-Oct Tue-Sat 10am-4pm, Nov-Apr Tue-Fri 10am-4pm, also by appointment.
Admission: Donations accepted. *Site Info:* On-site parking. Wheelchair accessible. Guides available. *Events:* Holiday Open House (Dec).
This 4-acre campus includes the main museum, Nichols/Beverly Agricultural Barn, Print Shop, Carter Barn, and Centennial Farmhouse and highlights the history of the Paw Paw Lakes area including Bainbridge Township, Coloma City, Coloma Township, Hagar Township, Watervliet City, and Watervliet Township. Exhibits feature resorts, fruit farming, businesses, industries, and area people.

Comstock Park

Alpine Township Historical Museum
Location: 2048 7 Mile Rd. NW, Comstock Park, MI 49321.
Contact: (616) 784-1262, b.alt@alpinetwp.org, www.alpinetwp.org.
Mail: 5255 Alpine Ave. NW. *Hours:* 3rd Sun of month, 2-4pm, also by appointment. *Admission:* Free. *Site Info:* On-site parking. Wheelchair accessible. Guides available. *Events:* Honoring Veterans (3rd Sun Nov).
The Alpine Township Historical Commission, appointed by the township board, administers a museum housed in the 1860 township hall, restored in 1987. The museum's collection includes a miniature replica of the original building, photo galleries of over 300 township veterans, early settlers, one-room schools, furniture, and artifacts of pioneer families.

Concord

Mann House
Location: 205 Hanover St., Concord, MI 49237.
Contact: (517) 524-8943, www.michigan.gov/mannhouse.
Hours: Memorial Day to Labor Day Wed-Sun 9:30am-4:30pm.
Admission: Free. *Site Info:* Free parking. Grounds and carriage house are wheelchair accessible, historic home is not accessible to those unable to use stairs. Docent available.
In 1883, Daniel and Ellen Mann built this two-story home in the farming community of Concord. The late-Victorian building features plaster ceilings, unusual catch-release doorknobs, a marbleized slate fireplace, eight rooms of period furniture, restored flower and herb gardens, and a carriage house with carriages, sleighs, and other exhibits. Part of the Michigan Historical Museum System.

Coopersville

Coopersville Area Historical Society Museum
Loccation: 363 Main St., Coopersville, MI 49404.
Contact: (616) 997-6978, (616) 997-7240, historicalsoc@allcom.net, www.coopersville.com/museum. *Hours:* Sat 10am-4pm, Tue 3-8pm, Wed 10am-1pm. Aug to mid-Dec Sun 1:30-4:30pm, also by appointment.
Admission: Free. *Site Info:* Free parking. Wheelchair accessible. Guide available, group tours welcome. *Events:* Summerfest (Aug), Museum by Moonlight (Dec), call for info.
This volunteer operation of the Historical Society is housed in a former interurban railroad depot listed in the National Register of Historic Places. Extensive drugstore exhibit, full-size sawmill exhibit, railroad and interurban train items, early schoolroom, area history exhibits, and Grand Rapids, Grand Haven, and Muskegon Railway interurban car #8, *Merlin*. The Del Shannon Memorial located on museum ground.

Dearborn

Arab American National Museum
Location: 13624 Michigan Ave., Dearborn, MI 48126.
Contact: (313) 582-2266, ksilarski@access community.org, www.arabamerican museum.org. *Hours:* Wed-Sat 10am-6 pm, Sun 12-5pm. *Admission:* Adults $6, Students & Seniors $3, under 6 free, Sun free (donation). *Site Info:* Free parking in city lot N. of museum. Wheelchair accessible. Min. 8 people required for group tour ($4 students/seniors, $8 adults). *Events:* Film Festival, Global Thursdays, free diversity music festival *Concert of Colors* at the Max

M. Fisher Music Center in Detroit.

This museum hosts exhibits on Arab immigration to the U.S., Arab lifestyles in the U.S., and significant contributions made by Arab Americans. Two rotating galleries feature 3-4 new exhibitions each year. Permanent exhibits are constantly updated with new information.

Dearborn Historical Museum

Location: See below.
Contact: (313) 565-3000, www.cityofdearborn.org/play/local-media/266-historical. *Mail:* 915 S. Brady, Dearborn, MI 48124. *Admission:* Both sites free. *Events:* Monthly lecture series, Then and Now school program, Victorian Tea, Garden Party Tea, History Hill (during homecoming), Fall into Dearborn.

Supported by the Museum Guild of Dearborn, the City of Dearborn's Local History Museum consists of three historic structures and a records archive. The museum has two campuses within two blocks of each other with multiple buildings:

1833 Commandant's Quarters

Location: 21950 Michigan Ave., Dearborn, MI 48124.
Contact: (313) 565-0844. *Hours:* Tue-Fri 11am-4pm.
Site Info: Metered parking. Not wheelchair accessible.
Commandant's Quarters has been restored to 1833-1875 time period and houses period rooms from the era. Exhibits depict Arsenal military history.

McFadden-Ross House

Location: 915 Brady St.
Hours: Tue-Fri 9am-4pm, Sat by appointment. *Site Info:* On-site free parking. Wheelchair accessible. *Events:* History Hill at Dearborn's Homecoming, Pioneer Days school program, Victorian Christmas Tea, Antique Appraisal Clinic (Oct), and Quilt Show.
Originally the 1839 powder magazine of Detroit Arsenal in Dearbornville, the structure was purchased by the Nathaniel Ross family in 1889 and converted to a farm house. House includes period rooms and extensive changing exhibit cases centered on Dearborn's history.

Floyd and Mary Haight Archives

Location: 2nd floor of the McFadden-Ross House.
Hours: Mon-Fri 9am-4pm, Sat by appointment.
Collection includes Dearborn-area genealogy records, 1820-1920 census records, yearbooks from area schools, Polk Directories from 1928 to present, local newspaper collection from 1905, photographs of Dearborn, and local history artifacts.

1831 Richard Gardner House

Hours: Open by request. *Site Info:* Wheelchair accessible.
This 1813 farmhouse of the Nathaniel Gardner family was moved to the site in 1996 where the three-room structure gives visitors a glimpse of Dearborn during simpler times. Features early American furnishings.

The Henry Ford

Location: 20900 Oakwood Blvd., Dearborn, MI 48124.
Contact: (313) 982-6001, www.thehenryford.org. *Hours:* Daily 9:30am-5pm, closed Thanksgiving and Christmas. *Admission:* Call or see website

for current ticket options for each location. *Site Info:* On-site parking. Wheelchair accessible. *Events:* Motor Muster Weekend, Day Out with Thomas, Salute to America, Civil War Remembrance, Old Car Festival, Historic Baseball, Halloween in Greenfield Village, Holiday Nights. Founded by Henry Ford in 1929 as the Edison Institute, The Henry Ford is the history attraction that brings the American experience to life. Major collections concern the history and cultural impact of the automobile, industrial manufacturing and design, and many other aspects of American culture. Exhibits include Automobile in American Life, With Liberty and Justice For All, Dymaxion House, Heroes of the Sky, and Presidential Limousines.

Greenfield Village
Hours: Daily Mid-Apr to Oct 9:30am-5pm, Nov-Dec Fri-Sun 9:30-5pm, closed Christmas.
Over forty historic industrial and residential structures in seven neighborhoods.

Ford Rouge Factory Tour
Hours: Mon-Sat 9:30am-5pm, last tour leaves 3pm. Call or check website to confirm schedule.
Self-guided five-part experience includes: Legacy Theater, Art of Manufacturing Theater, Observation Deck, Dearborn Truck Plant, and the Legacy Gallery.

Benson Ford Research Center
Hours: Mon-Fri 9am-5pm, closed major holidays, for appointment call (313) 982-6020.
Over 26 million archival, photographic, graphic, and print materials relating to the automobile industry, innovation, and historical and social development.

Decatur

Newton House
Location: 20689 Marcellus Hwy, Decatur, MI 49045-9455.
Contact: (269) 445-2907. *Hours:* May-Oct 1st Sun of month 1-4:30pm, also by appointment. *Site Info:* On-site parking.
This furnished, restored, mid-19th century Quaker home is owned by Michigan State University and maintained by the Cass County Historical Commission.

Detroit

Charles H. Wright Museum of African American History
Location: 315 E. Warren Ave., Detroit, MI 48201.
Contact: (313) 494-5800, tcanaday@chwmuseum.org, www.charleswrightmuseum.org. *Hours:* Tue-Sat: 9am-5pm, Sun 1-5pm.
Admission: Members free, Adults $8; Youth (3-12) & Seniors (62+) $5.
Site Info: Metered street parking or $5/day for rear lot. Wheelchair accessible. Guided tours $30. *Events:* Martin Luther King, Jr. Day (Jan), Black History Month (Feb), Women's History Month (March), Ford Freedom Awards (May), Black Music Month (Jun), African World

Festival (Aug), Grandparents Day (Sep), Noel Night (Dec), Kwanza Celebration (Dec).

The Charles H. Wright Museum of African American History provides learning opportunities, exhibitions, programs, and events based on collections and research that explore the diverse history and culture of African Americans and their African origins. The museum is the largest of its kind and strives to be recognized as the institution of choice for exploring and presenting African American history and culture. The museum houses more than 30,000 artifacts and archival materials and is the home to the Blanche Coggin Underground Railroad Collection, Harriet Tubman Museum Collection, Coleman A. Young Collection, and the Horace Sheffield Collection. The core exhibition is a 22,000 sq. ft. interactive experience titled, "And Still We Rise: Our Journey Through African American History and Culture."

Detroit Historical Museum

Location: 5401 Woodward Ave., Detroit, MI 48202.
Contact: (313) 833-7935, peterp@detroithistorical.org, www.detroithistorical.org. *Mail:* 5401 Woodward Ave., Detroit, MI 48202. *Hours:* Wed-Fri 9:30am-3pm, Sat 10am-5pm, Sun 12-5pm.
Admission: Adults $6, Seniors/Students $4, Children under 4 free. *Site Info:* Parking $14 per car. Wheelchair accessible. *Events:* African American History Day, Egg-stravaganza, Detroit's Birthday Party (Jul), Treats in the Streets (Oct), Noel Night (Dec).

Established in 1921, the Detroit Historical Society's mission is to educate and inspire its community and visitors by preserving and portraying its region's shared history through dynamic exhibits and experiences. The society is responsible for the overall management and operations of the Detroit Historical Museum. Exhibits include Frontiers to Factories, Motor City, New to the Collection, Streets of Old Detroit, the Glancy Trains, Doorway to Freedom, and the Detroit Artists Showcase.

Dossin Great Lakes Museum

Location: 100 Strand Dr. on Belle Isle.
Contact: (313) 833-5538. *Hours:* Sat-Sun 11am-4pm.
Admission: Free. *Site Info:* Free parking. Wheelchair accessible.
Exhibits include City on the Straits, Gothic Room, and the S.S. William Clay Ford Pilot House.

Motown Museum

Location: 2648 W. Grand Blvd., Detroit, MI 48208.
Contact: (313) 875-2264, kasmith@motownmuseum.org, www.motownmuseum.org.
Hours: Tue-Sat 10am-6pm, also Mon 10am-6pm in July.
Admission: Adults $10, Seniors/ Children 12 & under $8. *Site Info:* Free street parking. Wheelchair accessible. Guided tours available until 5pm.

Since 1985, the Motown Museum has been dedicated to preserving the legacy of Motown Records Corporation through the conservation of Motown's original site in Detroit and through exhibitions and programs.

Dexter

Dexter Area Historical Society and Museum
Location: 3443 Inverness St., Dexter, MI 48130.
Contact: (734) 426-2519, dexmuseum@aol.com,
www.hvcn.org/info/dextermuseum. *Hours:* May-Dec Fri-Sat 1-3pm, also
by appointment. *Admission:* Donations accepted. *Site Info:* On-site
parking. Wheelchair accessible. Guides available. *Events:* Dexter's
Pioneer Arts Fair (Mar), Holiday Fundraiser (Dec).
The museum, located in an 1883 church building, hosts displays of area
history with furniture, period clothing, toys, medical equipment, a
dentist's office, military artifacts from the Civil War to WWII, a carriage,
farm implements, school materials, and a model railroad layout
replicating the village of Dexter.

Dowagiac

Southwestern Michigan College Museum
Location: 58900 Cherry Grove Rd., Dowagiac, MI 49047.
Contact: (269) 782-1374, museum@swmich.edu,
www.swmich.edu/museum. *Hours:* Tue-Fri 10am-5pm, Sat 11am-3pm.
Admission: Free. *Site Info:* On-site parking. Wheelchair accessible.
Self-guided.
This museum presents local history exhibits focusing on Cass County,
aviation hero-Ivan Kincheloe, and the Round Oak Stove and Heddon Bait
Companies of Dowagiac.

Durand

Michigan Railroad History Museum
Location: 200 Railroad St., Durand, MI 48429.
Contact: (989) 288-3561, dusi@durandstation.org,
www.durandstation.org. *Mail:* P.O. Box 106. *Hours:* Tue-Sun 1-5pm,
archives and research library by appointment. *Admission:* Free.
Site Info: On-site parking. Wheelchair accessible. Guides available, group
tours by appointment. *Events:* Railroad Days (May).
Durand Union Station houses the Michigan Railroad History Museum,
incorporating the unique railroad heritage of Michigan and of the Durand
area. The museum collects, preserves, and interprets artifacts, records, and
documents related to the history of railroads and railroading in Michigan
and engages in activities that encourage interest in the railroad industry.

East Jordan

East Jordan Portside Art and Historical Museum
Location: 01656 S. M-66. East Jordan, MI 49727.
Contact: (231) 536-2250, kprebble@ejps.org, www.portsideartsfair.org.

Mail: P.O. Box 1355. *Hours:* Jun & Sep Sat-Sun 1:30-4:30pm. Jul-Aug Tue, Thu, & Sat-Sun 1:30-4:30pm. *Admission:* Donations accepted. *Site Info:* Free parking. Wheelchair accessible. Self-guided. *Events:* Portside Arts Fair (Aug).

Elm Pointe, originally the site of a pioneer homestead, became an 11-acre estate with a residence and lodge. Granted to the city by owners Dr. and Mrs. George Westgate in 1972, the main floor of the lodge now houses the museum with artifacts from the lumbering era, an agricultural exhibit, E.J. & Southern Railroad memorabilia, sa alute to the military and local manufacturing, and new annual exhibits. Adjacent to the museum is the Cygred Riley Art Gallery with collection of Purchase Prize paintings from annual Portside Arts Fair. Additional historical displays in the East Jordan City Hall (Mon-Fri 8am-5pm) include photos, families, ethnic genealogies, and early businesses.

East Lansing

Michigan State University Museum
Location: 103 Museum, East Lansing, MI 48824.
Contact: (517) 355-2370, news@museum.msu.edu, www.museum.msu.edu. *Hours:* Mon-Fri 9am-5pm, Sat 10am-5pm, Sun 1-5pm, closed University holidays. *Admission:* Free. *Site Info:* Parking in front of building $1 for two hour permit. Wheelchair accessible.
Events: Great Lakes Folk Festival (Aug), Chocolate Party Benefit (Feb), Dinosaur Dash (Oct), Darwin Discovery Day natural history program (Feb).

Started in 1857, the museum's long-term exhibits include Heritage Hall with displays on the Michigan fur trade, a country store, and a print shop. Partnership programs are run with the Michigan Native American Arts Initiative and the Michigan Traditional Arts Program.

East Tawas

Tawas Point Lighthouse
Location: Tawas Pt. State Park, 686 Tawas Beach Rd., East Tawas, MI 48730.
Contact: www.michigan.gov/tawaslighthouse, *Hours:* Memorial Day to Labor Day Wed-Sun 10am-5pm. *Admission:* $2 per person, funds restoration and exhibits. *Site Info:* State Park Motor Vehicle Permit required to enter park. Not wheelchair accessible. Self-guided.

In operation since 1876, the lighthouse and lighthouse keeper's quarters are undergoing continuing restoration. Part of the Michigan Historical Museum System.

Edwardsburg

Edwardsburg Museum
Location: 26818 Main St., Edwardsburg, MI 49112.
Contact: (616) 663-8408, JoBoepple@aol.com,
www.edwardsburg.biz/museum. *Mail:* P.O. Box 694. *Hours:* May-Dec
Tue-Fri 1-4pm, Sat 10am-2pm. Also Mon 1-4 May-Sep.
Admission: Donations accepted. *Site Info:* Parking across street and in
front of museum. Wheelchair accessible. Self-guided. *Events:* Plant sale,
US 12 Yard Sale, annual school reunion ice cream social, Flag Retirement
Ceremony, Witches on the Porch, Christmas Candy Sale.
This museum preserves and protects the history, heritage, and ancestry of
the Edwardsburg area. Collection includes artifacts, historical
photographs and documents from residents, clubs, organizations, schools,
and businesses from the townships of Ontwa, Jefferson, Milton and
Mason, and the village of Edwardsburg.

Elk Rapids

Elk Rapids Area Historical
Musuem
Location: 401 River St.,
Elk Rapids, MI 49629.
Contact: (231) 264-5692,
leblond@charter.net,
www.elkrapidshistory.org.
Mail: P.O. Box 2.

Hours: Memorial Day to Labor Day Tue, Thurs, & Sat-Sun 1-4pm, also
by appointment (call 231-264-8984). *Admission:* Donations accepted.
Site Info: Public parking on River St. and Spruce St. Not wheelchair
accessible. Guided tour by appointment. *Events:* Monthly programs May-
Nov, see website.
The museum is operated by the Elk Rapids Area Historical Society which
preserves, protects, and exhibits collections pertaining to the history of the
Chain of Lakes region, the village of Elk Rapids, its people, and
community life. Exhibits focus on Elk Rapids' role in the 19th-20th
centuries as an important lumbering, cement, chemical, and pig iron
smelting center.

Empire

Empire Area Museum Complex
Location: 11544 LaCore Rd., Empire, MI 49630.
Contact: (231) 326-5568, www.leelanau.cc/. *Mail:* P.O. Box 192.
Hours: Memorial Day to Jun Sat-Sun 1-4pm, Jul-Aug Sun-Tue & Thurs-
Sat 1-4pm, Labor Day to Oct Sat-Sun 1-4pm. *Admission:* Suggested
donation: $2 per person, $5 family. *Site Info:* On-site parking. Partially
wheelchair accessible. Volunteer docents. *Events:* Heritage Day (Oct).

The museum complex, administered by the Empire Area Heritage Group, includes the main museum, a one-room school house, a barn with horse-drawn equipment, and a 1911 vintage hose house (firehouse).

Essexville

Heritage House Farm Museum
Location: 503 Pine St., Essexville, MI 48732.
Contact: (989) 893-6186, pranspaugh@yahoo.com, *Mail:* P.O. Box 103.
Hours: Summer Sun 2-4pm, also by appointment. *Admission:* Donations accepted. *Site Info:* Nearby parking. Self-guided, guided tours available.
Events: Michigan History Elementary Schools Emphasis (Spring).
A fully furnished, nine-room home from the early 1890s, the home's only residents were members of John Garber family who built the house. Furniture within the home is a mixture of Garber family belongings and community artifacts collected over time. The site also includes a unique German-style shed, spring house, corn crib, and an herb garden. A volunteer group preserves the home for future generations.

Evart

Evart Public Library Museum
Location: 104 N. Main St., Evart, MI 49631.
Contact: (231) 734-5542. *Mail:* P.O. Box 576. *Hours:* Mon-Fri 9am-4 pm, Sat 9am-12:30pm. *Admission:* Free. *Site Info:* Street parking. Wheelchair accessible. Docent available part-time. *Events:* Annual Open House and Victorian Tea (Jun).
This local history museum in the public library features exhibits reflecting the history of the area and the interests of area citizens.

Fairview

Steiner Museum
Location: 1980 Reber Rd., Fairview, MI 48621.
Contact: (989) 255-9969, www.steinermuseum.org. *Hours:* Mid-May to Oct 1st Fri-Sun of the month 12-4 pm, also by appointment.
Admission: Donations accepted. *Site Info:* On-site parking. Wheelchair accessible. Self-guided. *Events:* Pancake Social (May), Quilt Show (June), Antique Appraisals (Jul), Heritage Days (Aug), Gun Show (Sep).
The Steiner Museum tells the history of Earl Steiner through an extensive collection of household artifacts from the early 20th century. Located in a log-sided frame building with an 1890 log school house and an extensive collection of early lumbering and farming equipment on the grounds.

Farmington Hills

Holocaust Memorial Center
Location: Zekelman Family Campus, 28123 Orchard Lake Rd.,
Farmington Hills, MI 48334.
Contact: (248) 553-2400, info@holocaustcenter.org,
www.holocaustcenter.org. *Hours:* Sun-Thurs 9:30am-5pm; Fri 9:30am-
3pm (last admission Sun-Thurs 3:30, Fri 12:30). Closed Sat & Jewish
holidays. *Admission:* Suggested donation $10 Adults, $4 Children.
Site Info: Wheelchair accessible. Public tours Sun-Thurs 1pm,
reservations for groups of six or more. *Events:* City-Wide Holocaust
Commemoration, International Symposium on Altruism.
The first free-standing US holocaust memorial when opened 1984, the
Memorial Center hosts speakers, educators conferences, lecture series,
and the International Institute of the Righteous. Museum tells the story of
Jewish heritage, the tragedy of the Holocaust, and the aftermath.

Farwell

Farwell Area Historical Museum
Location: 221 West Main St., Farwell, MI 48622.
Contact: (989) 544-2898, trishtom68@yahoo.com,
www.farwellmuseum.com. *Mail:* P.O. Box 824. *Hours:* Thurs-Fri 12-4
pm, also Sat 12-4pm in summer. *Admission:* Free. *Site Info:* Street
parking. Wheelchair acessible. Guides available. *Events:* Farwell
Lumberjack Days pancake breakfast (Jul), Holiday of Lights (Nov).
Located in the 1882 Ladies Library Association building shared with the
Chamber of Commerce, the mususem hosts exhibits highlighting local
history including a school, mill, post office, and local figures.

Ferndale

Ferndale Historical Museum
Location: 1651 Livernois,
Ferndale, MI 48220.
Contact: (248) 545-7606,
garryandrewsmich@comcast.net,
www.ferndalehistoricalsociety.org.
Hours: Mon & Wed 10am-1pm,
Sat 1-4pm. *Admission:* Donations
accepted. *Site Info:* On-site parking. Partially wheelchair accessible.
Docents available. *Events:* Memorial Day and Veterans Day Open House
Meet and Greets.
The museum is housed in a building given to the city by Canadian Legion
Post No. 71. Its collections date from the 19th century including a large
military installation covering all of America's greatest wars and a study of
the histories of all 8,000 structures in Ferndale.

Fife Lake

Fife Lake Historical Museum
Location: 136 E. State St., Fife Lake, MI 49633.
Contact: (231) 879-3342, www.fifelake.com/history/index.htm.
Mail: P.O. Box 305. *Hours:* Memorial Day to Labor Day, call for hours.
Admission: Free. *Site Info:* On-site parking. Wheelchair accessible.
Guides available. *Events:* 4th of July Buffalo BBQ.
The Fife Lake Area Historical Society was organized in 1967 to provide
displays of local history and prehistory. Nearby are the Fife Lake
Historical Fire Barn with a 1936 fire truck, uniforms, and large wheeled
fire-fighting equipment, and an 1878 one-room school.

Flat Rock

Flat Rock Historical Museum
Location: 25200 Gibraltar Rd., Flat Rock, MI 48134.
Contact: (734) 782-5220, dcfesko@yahoo.com, www.flatrockhistory.org.
Mail: P.O. Box 337. *Hours:* 2nd Sunday of month 1-4pm.
Admission: Free. *Site Info:* Parking in Flat Rock Library lot. Partially
wheelchair accessible. Docents present, group tours by appointment.
Events: Flea market (May & Oct), Flat Rock Speedway.
The Flat Rock Historical Society, formed 1975 to save the Munger
General Store, now maintains historic buildings as a local museum.
Buildings maintained include the C.J. Munger Store (1875), Flat Rock
Hotel (1896), Carriage House (1860), DTI Caboose (1926), and the
unrestored Wagar House (1875). Special exhibits change regularly.

Flint

Alfred P. Sloan Museum
Location: 1221 E. Kearsley St.,
Flint, MI 48503.
Contact: (810) 237-3450,
tshickles@sloanlongway.org,
www.sloanmuseum.org.
Hours: Museum Mon-Fri 10am-
5pm, Sat-Sun 12-5pm. Business
hours Mon-Fri 8am-5pm.
Admission: Adults $6, youth
(ages 4-11) $5. *Site Info:* On-site parking. Wheelchair accessible. Self-
guided. *Events:* Auto Fair (Jun), Car Show (Sep), Holiday Walk.
A museum of regional history, historic automobiles, and hands-on science
whose collection includes an operating 1940s soda fountain from
Mackenzie's Drug Store and 100,000 artifacts ranging from prehistoric
stone implements to antique textiles and prototype automobiles. The
Science Discovery Center allows exploration of the principles of
chemistry and physics while the Hometown Gallery invites exploration of
the 19th century with interactive hands-on activities in three historic

settings. The Pierson Automotive Gallery hosts major automotive exhibits featuring vehicles from the Sloan fleet of over 80 Flint-built automobiles. The area's tumultuous 20th century history is portrayed in the exhibit "Flint and the American Dream."

Buick Gallery and Research Center
Location: 303 N. Walnut St.
Contact: (810) 237-3440. *Hours:* Gallery open Mon-Fri 10-5, Sat 12-5. Archives by appointment only, call ahead.
The Buick Gallery contains 25 classic and concept Buicks, Chevrolets, and other locally built automobiles. The Perry Archives house a collection of photographs and papers that document Flint and Genesee County history, Buick engineering papers, service manuals, sales literature, and cemetery/funeral home records. Researchers can view information in the reading room by appointment, Flint Genealogical Society volunteers assist researchers Wed 10am-3pm.

Whaley House Museum
Location: 624 E. Kearsley St., Flint, MI 48503.
Contact: (810) 235-6841, 1885@whaleyhouse.com, www.whaleyhouse.com.
Hours: Tours Tue, Thurs-Fri 10am & 3pm, Sat 1-4pm.
Admission: Adults $5, Students $3.
Site Info: On-site parking. Partially wheelchair accessible: first floor only. Guided tours.

Events: Christmas at Whaley House Museum.
This Late Victorian era home depicts life at the turn of the 19th-20th centuries in Flint. Listed in the National Register of Historic Places.

Flushing

Flushing Area Museum and Cultural Center
Location: 431 W. Main St, Flushing, MI 48433.
Contact: (810) 487-0814, fahs@att.net, www.flushinghistorical.org.
Hours: Tue 9am-1pm, also Sun 1-4pm in Apr-Dec and by appointment. Closed holiday weekends. *Admission:* Free. *Site Info:* Free parking. Wheelchair accessible. Self-guided. *Events:* Candlewalk (Dec).
This restored 1888 Grand Trunk depot now hosts a museum with displays on railroading, local history, veterinary medical equipment, drugstore items, and 1930s kitchen appliances.

Frankenmuth

Frankenmuth Historical Museum
Location: 613 S. Main, Frankenmuth, MI 48734.
Contact: (989) 652-9701, fhadirector@airadv.net, www.frankenmuthmuseum.org. *Hours:* Mon-Thurs 10:30am-5pm, Fri

10:30am-8pm, Sat 10am-8pm, Sun 11am-7pm. Hours may vary by season. *Admission:* Adults $2, Students $1, Family pass $5. *Site Info:* Free parking. Wheelchair accessible. Self-guided, guides available by reservation. *Events:* Fundraising Auction (Nov).
This museum in the 1905 Kern Commercial House Hotel preserves and communicates area heritage from the Franconian community's original 15 settlers to today's "Little Bavaria," one of Michigan's top tourist destinations. Museum includes a 7-gallery permanent exhibit with additional temporary exhibits.

Franklin

Franklin Historical Museum
Location: 26165 13 Mile Rd., Franklin, MI 48025.
Contact: (248) 538-0565, www.franklin-history.org. *Mail:* P.O. Box 250007. *Hours:* Sat 1-3pm, also by appointment. *Admission:* Free.
Site Info: Free parking.
The Franklin Historical Society preserves and protects objects, sites, and buildings which are of interest in the history of Franklin. The museum is located in a 1951 ranch home donated by the Derwich family.

Gagetown

Friends of the Thumb Octagon Barn
Location: 6948 Richie Rd., Gagetown, MI 48735.
Contact: (989) 665-0081, www.thumboctagonbarn.org. *Mail:* P.O. Box 145. *Hours:* Daily May-Oct 8am-8pm. *Admission:* Donations accepted.
Site Info: Free parking. Self-guided. *Events:* School tours (May), Fall Family Days (Sep).
This 70-foot-high 8,000+ square foot Octagon Barn was part of "Mud Lake Estate" built by banker James Purdy in the 1920s. The Friends are a volunteer group committed to its preservation and to the interpretation of rural life. Site includes the Craftsman-style Purdy home and a one-room school.

Galesburg

Galesburg Historical Museum
Location: 188-1/2 E. Michigan Ave., Galesburg, MI 49053.
Contact: (269) 665-9011, (269) 665-7191. *Hours:* Wed 3-7:30pm, Sat 10am-2pm. Also by appointment, call (269)-665-9953.
Admission: Donations accepted. *Site Info:* On-site parking. Wheelchair accessble. Self-guided, guided tours available with advance notice.
Events: Open annually for Greater Galesburg Day.
Volunteers maintain this museum, with exhibits of local and military history, and a 4-room home c. 1860 with a kitchen, parlor, dining room, and bedroom.

Garden City

Garden City Historical Museum
Location: 6221 Merriman Rd., Garden City, MI 48135.
Contact: (734) 838-0650, straight.farmhouse@yahoo.com,
www.sfhonline.org. *Hours:* Wed & Sat 12-3pm. *Admission:* Donations
accepted. *Site Info:* Free parking. Wheelchair accessible. Free guide.
This local history museum is located in the historic Straight Farmhouse.
See website for current exhibit information.

Gaylord

Otsego County Historical Museum
Location: 320 W. Main St., Gaylord, MI 49734.
Contact: (989) 732-4568, ochsmuseum@gmail.com,
www.otsego.org/ochs. *Mail:* P.O. Box 1223. *Hours:* Jun to Labor Day
Mon-Tue & Thurs-Sat 10am-4pm. Labor Day to Oct Thu-Sat 10am-4pm.
Admission: Free. *Site Info:* On-site parking. Wheelchair accessible. Self-
guided. *Events:* Antique Appraisal (Sep).
Administered by the Otsego County Historical Society, the museum
maintains a collection of artifacts displayed in a 1911 cigar factory
building. Exhibits feature lumbering, farming, furniture, commerce, and
the Dayton Lost Block Works of Gaylord.

Gladwin

Gladwin County Historic Village
Location: 221 W. Cedar Ave., Gladwin, MI 48624.
Contact: (989) 426-7410, tcummins@ejourney.com,
www.gladwinhistory.org. *Hours:* Memorial Day to Labor Day Fri-Sat 1-
4pm. *Admission:* Free. *Site Info:* Free parking. Self-guided.
Events: Opening Day, Log Cabin Day (Jun), Carriage Festival, Founder's
Day (Oct).
This museum complex features a restored Michigan Central Railroad
depot with seven other buildings. The collection includes a carriage house
c. 1890 with a carriage and a cutter collection at the fairgrounds.

Grand Blanc

Grand Blanc Heritage Association Museum
Location: 203 E. Grand Blanc Rd., Grand Blanc, MI 48439.
Contact: (810) 694-7274, dharrett@tir.com, www.cityofgrandblanc.com.
Hours: Wed 10am-2pm, also by appointment. *Admission:* Donations
accepted. *Site Info:* Parking in city lot. Limited wheelchair accessibility.
Guided tours available by appointment. *Events:* Memorial Day Open
House, Old Fashioned Christmas Program.

The museum, located in an 1885 church building, preserves the history of Grand Blanc and its surrounding area. Two floors of exhibits are available for viewing

Grand Haven

Tri-Cities Historical Museum

Location: 200 Washington Ave, Grand Haven, MI 49417.
Contact: (616) 842-0700, dswartout@tri-citiesmuseum.org, www.tri-citiesmuseum.org.
Hours: Summer Tue-Fri 9:30am-7:30pm & Sat-Sun 12:30-7:30
pm, winter Tue-Fri 9:30am-5pm & Sat-Sun 12:30-5pm. *Admission:* Free. *Site Info:* On-site free parking. Wheelchair accessible. Free guided group tours available by appointment. *Events:* Feast of Strawberry Moon 18th century living history event (Aug).

Housed in a restored 1871 downtown store building, the museum hosts permanent and rotating exhibits giving a chronological history of the Tri-Cities area. Exhibits highlight Michigan geology, Native Americans, lumbering, pioneer living, industry, farming, and Victorian living.

Depot Transportation Museum
Location: 1 N. Harbor Dr.
This museum in the 1870 Detroit & Milwaukee depot showcases the history of railroading, automobiles, and bicycles.

Grand Ledge

Grand Ledge Museum
Location: 118 W. Lincoln St., Grand Ledge, MI 48837.
Contact: (517) 627-3149, arnor1@comcast.net, www.gdledgehistsoc.org.
Mail: P.O. Box 203. *Hours:* Sun 2-4pm, Festival Days 12-4pm, also by appointment. *Admission:* Donations accepted. *Site Info:* Free street or lot parking. Wheelchair accessible. Guided tours available, contact museum for information and prices. *Events:* Color Cruise and Island Festival (Oct), Holiday Traditions Tour (Dec).

This museum of local history, administered by the Grand Ledge Area Historical Society, is located in the 1880 Gothic Revival Pratt-Shearer Cottage. Themed special exhibits change annually. Displays include Grand Ledge Chair Co. furniture and other local artifacts. The society is also involved with the historic preservation of the local opera house.

Grand Ledge Opera House
Location: 121 S. Bridge St., Grand Ledge, MI 48837.
Contact: (517) 627-1443, arnor1@comcast.net, www.gdledgehistsoc.org.
Hours: Mon-Fri 9am-5pm. *Admission:* Free. *Site Info:* On-site parking. Wheelchair accessible. Guided tours available.

Beautifully restored in the Victorian style, the Grand Ledge Opera House is home to the Grand Ledge Area Chamber of Commerce and is open for tours during the Chamber's normal business hours. Built during the 1880s as the Riverside Rink, it was soon converted to Blake's Opera House and was later used to show early silent films. During the late 1920s, the Opera House was converted to a furniture store and served as the headquarters for Mapes Furniture. The main floor now houses an antique Barton Theater organ.

Grand Rapids

Cascade History Room
Location: Cascade Township Library, 2870 Jack Smith Ave. SE, Grand Rapids, MI 49546.
Contact: (616) 868-6465, morningspirit@comcast.net. *Hours:* Open during library hours. *Admission:* Free. *Site Info:* Wheelchair accessible. Guide available Thurs 1-3pm.
Features displays of Cascade history by the Cascade Historical Society.

Gerald R. Ford Presidential Museum

Location: 303 Pearl St. NW, Grand Rapids, MI 49504.
Contact: (616) 254-0400, kristin.mooney@nara.gov, www.fordlibrarymuseum.gov. *Hours:* Daily 9am-5pm. *Admission:* Call or see website for admission rates. *Site Info:* Free parking. Wheelchair accessible. Self-guided.
Events: See website.
The museum, along with the Gerald R. Ford Presidential Library (archives) in Ann Arbor, comprises a unit of the National Archives and Records Administration system of presidential libraries. Collections and exhibits related to the life and presidency of Gerald R. Ford, 38th president of the United States, include artifacts and interactive displays.

Grand Rapids Public Library History Collections
Location: 111 Library NE, Grand Rapids, MI 49503.
Contact: (616) 988-5402, localhis@grpl.org, www.grhistory.org.
Hours: Mon-Thurs 9am-9pm, Fri-Sat 9am-5:30pm, also Labor Day to Memorial Day Sun 1-5pm.
The Grand Rapids Historical Society collects and preserves local history materials and promotes local history through public programs and publications, using space in the Grand Rapids Public library and the Gerald R. Ford Presidential Museum. The Society had collection of over 30,000 items when Ryerson Library was built in 1904. A history room was created and the relationship continues through the Grand Rapids History and Special Collections section of the library.

Public Museum of Grand Rapids

Location: 272 Pearl St. NW, Grand Rapids, MI 49504.
Contact: (616) 456-3977, info@grmuseum.org, www.grmuseum.org.
Hours: Mon-Sat 9am-5pm, Sun 12-5pm. Closed Thanksgiving,
Christmas, New Year's. *Admission:* Adults $8, Seniors $7, Youth (3-17)
$3. *Site Info:* Parking ramp across the street half price with admission.
Wheelchair accessible. *Events:* Front Row for Fireworks (Jul), Pow-Wow
Along the Owashtinong (Fall), Ethnic Heritage Festival (Winter), Night at
Your Museum (Winter).
Founded in 1854, this non-profit educational institution operates
Michigan's oldest and third largest museum. The museum collects,
preserves, and presents the natural, cultural, and social history of the
region. Permanent exhibits include: Streets of Old Grand Rapids,
Collecting A to Z, Anishinabek: People of This Place, Habitats, Furniture
City, and Newcomers.

Voigt House Victorian Museum

Location: 115 College Ave. SE.
Contact: (616) 456-4600, cham@grcity.us. *Hours:* Tue 11am-3pm,
2nd & 4th Sun of month 1-3pm. Business hours Mon-Fri 9am-4pm.
Admission: Adults $3, Seniors & Youth (ages 6-17) $2.
Site Info: Group tours, weddings, and meals by reservation.
Events: German fest (Oct), Victorian Christmas program (Nov-Jan).
This historic 1895 Heritage Hill home of the Voigts, a prominent
merchant and flour mill family, contains the Voigt family's original
furnishings and personal possessions.

Grandville

Grandville Historical Commission Museum

Location: City Hall, 3195 Wilson Ave. SW, Grandville, MI 49418.
Contact: (616) 531-3030, grandvillehistorical@iserv.net. *Mail:* P.O. Box
124. *Hours:* Jan-May & Sep-Nov 1st Thurs of month 7pm, also by
appointment. *Events:* #10 School Open House (Independence Day and
Labor Day weekends), school field trips (Spring).
The Commission, appointed by the city, manages the Museum Room in
City Hall and the 19th century, one-room #10 School located in Heritage
Park. The museum collection includes objects of local interest, an
extensive collection of photographs, an active oral history program with
senior citizens about the early history of their community, and scrapbooks
dating back to the 1900s.

Grass Lake

Waterloo Farm Museum

Location: 13493 Waterloo-Munith Rd., Grass Lake, MI 49240.
Contact: (517) 596-2254, www.waterloofarmmuseum.org. *Mail:* P.O.
Box 37, Stockbridge, MI 49285. *Hours:* Jun-Aug Fri-Sun 1-5pm, House
Sat-Sun June-Sep 1-5pm. *Admission:* Adults $3, Seniors $2.50, Youth $1,
grounds admission for Pioneer Day $2. *Events:* Pioneer Day (Oct),

Christmas on the Farm (Dec), Woodland Indian Living History (Jun), Blacksmith Festival (Jun), Michigan Log Cabin Day (Jun).

This complex includes the Realy Family homestead and the one-room Dewey School, one-room school, maintained to foster an understanding of pioneer farmers in Michigan, their family life, and schooling. Waterloo Area Historical Society volunteers give tours, living history interpretations, demonstrations, and craft classes.

Dewey School
Location: Corner of Territorial Rd. and Mayer Rd..
Hours: Open for special events and by appointment.
Restored one-room school operated 1844-1956. Living history programs for elementary students available in May, Jun, Sep, or Oct by appointment. Participants learn what life was like and get to help with a typical day's chores.

Whistlestop Depot
Location: 210 E. Michigan, Grass Lake, MI 49240.
Contact: (517) 522-4384, richlyns12@aol.com, jomac@yahoo.com, www.grasslakehistoricalrental.com. *Mail:* P.O. Box 202. *Hours:* Tours by appointment. *Admission:* Donations accepted. *Site Info:* Parking on Main Street. Wheelchair accessible. *Events:* Victorian Tea, Independence Day parade, Heritage Day (Sep), Holiday Open House (Dec).
The non-profit Whistlestop Park Association restored and developed the park to enhance historical and cultural Grass Lake and to promote tourism. The Victorian stone depot with Victorian gardens, a gazebo, and a train shed features displays of artwork and artifacts.

Grayling

Crawford County Museum
Location: 97 E. Michigan Ave., Grayling, MI 49738.
Contact: (989) 348-4461, www.grayling-area.com/museum. *Mail:* P.O. Box 218. *Hours:* Memorial Day to Oct Wed-Sat 10am-4pm.
Admission: Donations accepted. *Site Info:* On-site parking. Wheelchair accessible. Guides available. *Events:* Historic Home Tour, Cemetery Walk, Train Excursion (Oct).
This site features a large railroad display in the 1882 Michigan Central depot. The Au Sable River display includes a 1915 riverboat. Exhibit rooms show life as a trapper's wife, a seamstress, and a doctor, a school room, a grocery store, a saloon, Fred Bear memorabilia, a sheriff's display, and a photo display of Camp Grayling.

Hartwick Pines Logging Museum
Location: Hartwick Pines State Park, 4216 Ranger Rd., Grayling, MI 49738.
Contact: (989) 348-6178, www.michigan.gov/loggingmuseum.
Hours: Jun to Labor Day 9am-dusk, call for hours other times of year.
Admission: State Park Motor Vehicle Permit required. *Site Info:* On-site parking. Visitor center and logging museum are wheelchair accessible, Old-Growth Forest Trail is paved but includes two steep grades. Self-guided.

Situated within one of Michigan's largest stands of virgin white pine, the forest visitor center and logging camp buildings, exhibits, and period rooms tell the stories of the loggers, river men, and entrepreneurs who powered the white pine industry. Follow the Forest Trail to a 300-year-old monarch pine. Part of the Michigan Historical Museum System.

Lovells Township Historical Society Museums
Location: 8405 Twin Bridge Rd., Grayling, MI 49738.
Contact: (989) 348-4880, rogerfechner@aol.com. *Hours:* May-Sep Sat 10am-4pm, Jun-Aug Wed 10am-4pm Fri 4-8pm. *Admission:* Free.
Events: Trout Opener (Apr), "Bear, Beaver and Banjo" Fundraiser (Jul), Lovells Bridge Walk (Aug).
The society maintains two buildings: the 1907 Lone Pine School with House-Lovells community history and the Log Fishing Museum with the history of trout fishing on the North Branch of the Au Sable River.

Wellington Farm Park
Location: 6940 S. Military Rd., Grayling, MI 49738.
Contact: (888) 653-3276, (989) 348-5187, howard@i2k.net, www.wellingtonfarmpark.org. *Mail:* 6771 S. Military Rd. *Hours:* Daily May-Oct 9am-5pm. *Events:* Dairy Days (Jun), Sticky Buns (Jul), Tractor and Engine Show (Aug), Free Fair (Aug), Folk Art Festival (Sep), Haunting Wellington (Oct), Murder Mystery Shows.
At this working replica of mid-American farmstead during the 1930s, activities conducted daily use vintage equipment, tools, and practices. The site also features a complete program of environmental education. Stiltsville Church, the only building remaining in the logging town of Stiltsville, was moved to the farm and is undergoing restoration.

Grosse Ile

Michigan Central Railroad Depot Museum

Location: 25020 E. River Rd.
Contact: (734) 675-1250.
Mail: P.O. Box 131, Grosse Ile, MI 48138. *Hours:* Sun 1-4pm, Thurs 10am-12pm.
Admission: Free. *Site Info:* Free on-site parking. Not wheelchair accessible. Self-guided.
Organized in 1959, the Grosse Ile Historical Society preserves and presents Grosse Ile's history to the public. This museum located in a 1904 depot exhibits displays on railroads, community life, and significant Grosse Ile artifacts.

Custom House Museum
Location: 25020 E. River Rd.
The Custom House contains additional displays and the Grosse Ile Historical Society's archives.
Naval Airstation Grosse Ile
Location: Grosse Ile Township Hall, 9601 Groh Rd.

Hours: Mon-Fri 8am-5pm. *Admission:* Free. *Site Info:* Free on-site parking. Self-guided.

The Airstation exhibit examines naval history and celebrates Grosse Ile's legacy as a naval airstation through artifacts and photographs. Includes memorial garden.

Grosse Ile Light
Location: Lighthouse Point Rd.
Site Info: Not wheelchair accessible. Guided tour.

The 1894 lighthouse is open to the public once in Sep. for an annual tour.

Grosse Pointe Farms

Provencal-Weir House
Location: 376 Kercheval Ave, Grosse Pte. Farms, MI 48236.
Contact: (313) 884-7010, GPHistorical@aol.com, www.gphistorical.org.
Mail: GPHS Resource Center, 381 Kercheval Ave. *Hours:* Archives Tue-Wed 10am-12pm, 1:30-4:30pm. Provencal-Wier House Tours 2nd Sat of month, also by appointment.

This Greek Revival farmhouse is believed to be community's oldest surviving residence, built c. 1823 by Pierre Provencal. An 1840s log cabin is also located on the property.

Hamburg

Hamburg Historical Museum
Location: 7225 Stone St., Hamburg, MI 48139.
Contact: (810) 986-0190, suzanne@pendragon-design.com, www.hamburg.mi.us/hamburg_historical_museum/index.htm.
Mail: P.O. Box 272. *Hours:* Wed 4-7pm, Sat 11am-3pm.
Admission: Free. *Events:* Hamburg Festival and Railroad Days (Sep).

The museum opened in 2004 in a mid-1850s Methodist Church later used as the Hamburg Public Library. Exhibits change quarterly.

Hamtramck

Ukrainian American Archives and Museum
Location: 11756 Charest St., Hamtramck, MI 48212.
Contact: (313) 366-9764, ukrainianmuseum@sbcglobal.net, www.ukrainianmuseumdetroit.org. *Hours:* Mon-Fri 9am-5pm.
Admission: Free. *Site Info:* Free parking.

This museum opened in 1958 to educate and inform the general public about the culture, art, and history of Ukrainians, their immigration to the United States, and their contributions to America. The museum maintains an archives, acquires artifacts, and sponsors public programs.

Hanover

Hanover-Horton Museum
Location: 105 Fairview St.,
Hanover, MI 49241.
Contact: (517) 563-8927,
info@conklinreedorganmuseum.org,
www.conklinreedorganmuseum.org.
Mail: P.O. Box 256. *Hours:* May-
Oct Sun 1-5pm, also by appointment.
Admission: By donation. *Site Info:*
On-site parking. Partially wheelchair
accessible. Self-guided, guided group tours $3/person with reservation
(minimum 10 people, lunch option $7.50/person). *Events:* Plow Day
(Apr), Independence Day, Rust'N'Dust (Aug), Fall Festival (Sep).
The museum includes one of the largest collections of antique reed organs
and melodeons in the U.S. The collection also includes a restored
classroom, printing press, and Model-T popcorn truck. Organ restoration
workshops give hands-on training in reed organ repair and maintenance.

Heritage Park
Sitting on 82+ acres, this site is an agricultural showcase of early
farming techniques

Historic Hanover School
This school houses a collection of over 100 playable reed (pump)
organs, melodeons, and harmoniums.

Fire History Hall
Within the hall are restored antique fire apparatus and a 1950s era
water pump truck.

Harbor Beach

White Rock School Museum
Location: 10124 White Rock Rd., Harbor Beach, MI 48441.
Contact: (989) 864-5591, dicknor2@verizon.net, *Hours:* By appointment.
Admission: Donations accepted. *Site Info:* On-site free parking.
Wheelchair accessible. *Events:* Annual Picnic (Aug), Holiday
Party (Dec).
Housed in brick, one-room 1909 schoolhouse, the museum contains
printed material, photos, maps, and memorabilia that help establish or
illustrate the history of the school and its environs.

Harbor Springs

Harbor Springs History Museum
Location: 349 E. Main St., Harbor Springs, MI 49740.
Contact: (231) 526-9771, info@harborspringshistory.org,
www.harborspringshistory.org. *Mail:* P.O. Box 812. *Hours:* Open year-
round, call or see website hours. *Admission:* Adults $5, Seniors/Children

$3, HSAHS members free. *Site Info:* Limited on-site parking, ample street parking. Self-guided. Wheelchair accessible. *Events:* Call or see website.
The Harbor Springs Area Historical Society seeks to acquire, preserve, display, and study historical materials relating to the area surrounding Harbor Springs. The museum is housed in the former 1886 city hall building featuring exhibits, meeting space, and hands-on activities. Two permanent exhibit galleries detail the unique history of the Harbor Springs area and include an Odawa language activity, a model Shay locomotive, and more.

Harrisville

Sturgeon Point Lighthouse and Museum

Location: 6071 E. Sturgeon Pointe Rd. Harrisville, MI 48740.
Contact: (989) 727-4703, lklemens@ymail.com, www.alcona historicalsociety.com. *Mail:* P.O. Box 174. *Hours:* Weekends starting Memorial Day 11am-4pm, daily mid-June to Labor Day. Lighthouse tower Fri-Sun 11am-3:30pm. *Admission:* $3/person, $10 for four people. Visitors must be 42 inches tall to tour the lighthouse. *Site Info:* Free parking. Not wheelchair accessible. Self-guided. *Events:* Strawberry Social (Jun), Alcona History Day (Aug).
This 1869 Lighthouse was staffed until 1941. The Alcona Historical Society began restoration of the operating tower and site in 1982. The lighthouse keeper's home is now a maritime museum. The Society also maintains the Old Bailey School, a log one-room schoolhouse, and the Lincoln Train Depot (Depot open Mon-Fri 1-4pm).

Hart

Hart Historic District

Location: 100 Union St., Hart, MI 49420.
Contact: (231) 873-2488, www.ci.hart.mi.us. *Mail:* City of Hart, 407 State St. *Hours:* Jul-Aug, Wed-Sat 1-4pm. *Admission:* Adults $5, Children $2, Family $10, groups of 10+ $3/person. *Site Info:* Free parking. Wheelchair accessible. Free guide available. *Events:* Jul-Aug Concert Series, Heritage Days Festival, Labor Day weekend.
The Historic District is managed jointly by the Heritage Preservation Group and the Hart Historic District Commission. Buildings include: 1858 Native American log cabin (Cobmoosa House), 1868 Hart railroad depot, 1876 Randall School, 1897 Sackrider Church, 1917 Mudget Wood Shop, 1917 Wilde Blacksmith Shop (privately owned), 1920 Schaner Feed Mill, 1947 log house, 1993 B.R. Mudget Pavilion, 2002 Heritage Hall, 2005 heritage complex.

Oceana County Historical and Genealogical Society Research Library and Headquarters

Location: 114 Dryden St, Hart, MI 49420.
Contact: (231) 873-2600, info@oceanahistory.org, www.oceanahistory.org.
Hours: Wed 10am-5pm.
Admission: Free. *Site Info:* Free parking. Self-guided. *Events:* Postcard Show (Jun), Pleasant Afternoon (Aug).

The Oceana County Historical Society was organized in 1967 and the Chadwick-Munger House in Hart was acquired in 1984 for headquarters. Extensive historical and genealogical records for Oceana County are stored here including thousands of photographs of the area and of residents, many examples of the work of local artists, over 50,000 obituaries, a large number of indexed family histories, history books, and other publications of the society, and a file of over 500,000 names with indexed sources of information.

Hartford

Van Buren County Historical Society Museum

Location: 58471 Red Arrow Hwy., Hartford, MI 49057. *Contact:* (269) 621-2188. *Mail:* P.O. Box 452. *Hours:* Jun-Sep Wed & Fri-Sat 12-5pm, also by appointment. *Admission:* Adults $5, Children 12 & under $1.
Site Info: On-site parking. Partially wheelchair accessible. Docents available. *Events:* Demonstration Day, Yearly Antique Appraisal, No Guilt Show.

The society's museum is housed in the historic 1884 County Poorhouse. Three floors of historical items include a one-room school, a general store housing period products, a music room, an old-fashioned kitchen, a turn-of-the-century parlor, an old dentist office, a military room, and two revolving exhibit rooms. The site features a replica log cabin and blacksmith works on the grounds.

Hartland

Florence B. Dearing Museum

Location: 3503 Avon St., Hartland, MI 48353.
Contact: (810) 632-6711, nadinecloutier@comcast.net, tom@imcporducts.com, www.hartlandareahistory.org. *Mail:* P.O. Box 49.
Hours: Call or see website. *Admission:* $1/person donation. *Site Info:* On-site parking. Self-guided. *Events:* Annual Dinner (Feb).

The museum, administered by the Hartland Area Historical Society, in located in the former township hall and includes a rural farm kitchen, parlor, and items found in the home. Exhibits include a farm implement display, a collection of animals found in the area, a general store, and a textiles display showcasing the area as a leading weaving community from 1930s-40s.

Hastings

Historic Charlton Park Village
Location: 2545 S. Charlton Park Rd., Hastings, MI 49058.
Contact: (269) 945-3775, claire_l_Johnston@yahoo.com.
www.charltonpark.org. *Hours:* Daily Memorial Day to Labor Day Museum and Historic Village 9am-4pm, Recreation Area 8am-9pm. Off-season office hours Mon-Fri 8am-5pm. *Admission:* Free except during special events. *Site Info:* Self-guided. *Events:* Charlton Park Day, Father's Day Car Show, Independence Day BBQ, Gas and Steam Show, Civil War Muster, Walk in the Spirit Pow Wow, Lumberjack Show, Great Lakes Longbow Invitational, All Hallows Eve, Of Christmas Past.
This 20-building reconstructed rural village helps educate people in 19th century Barry County life through school programs for children, and 100,000 artifacts covering the lives of rural Michigan residents including agricultural equipment, vocational tools, furniture, textiles, housewares, firearms, gas and steam engines, and communication devices. Includes a recreation area for public use.

Hickory Corners

Gilmore Car Museum
Location: 6865 Hickory Rd., Hickory Corners, MI 49060.
Contact: (616) 671-5089, (269) 671-5089, info@gilmore carmuseum.org, www.gilmore carmuseum.org. *Hours:* May-Oct Mon-Fri 9am-5pm, Sat-Sun 9am-6pm. Wed Cruise-Ins at Blue Moon Diner 6-9pm. *Admission:* Adults $9, Seniors $8, Students (7-15) $7. *Site Info:* Free parking. Partially  wheelchair accessible. Large group tours available for a small fee. *Events:* See website for schedule of car shows.
This museum maintains a world-class collection of nearly 200 antique, classic, and collector cars from every era and taste. Exhibits range from an 1899 Locomobile to a classic Duesenberg, elusive Tucker '48, Model T, and the muscle cars of 1960s-70s. Situated on a 90-acre park-like setting with several historic Michigan barns, a 1930s gas station, and an operating 1940s diner.

Hillsdale

Hillsdale County Museum

Location: Hillsdale County Fairgrounds, 115 S. Broad St., Hillsdale, MI 49242.
Contact: (517) 437-4600, hchistoricalsociety1@yahoo.com. *Mail:* 3750 Duryea Ln. *Hours:* By appointment. *Admission:* Free. *Site Info:* On-site parking. Partially wheelchair accessible. Self-guided. *Events:* Civil War Days with 18th Michigan Regiment Re-enactors (Jun), Will Carleton Festival, Hillsdale County Fair (Sep), Christmas Open House (Dec). Contains exhibits of artifacts from Hillsdale County maintained by the Hillsdale County Historical Society.

Will Carleton Poorhouse Museum
Location: 180 N. Wolcott Rd.
This cobblestone house built in mid-1800s was once used as Hillsdale County's Poorhouse and as the basis for Will Carleton's poem "Over the Hill to the Poorhouse."

Holland

Holland Museum

Location: 31 W. 10th Street, Holland, MI 49423.
Contact: (616) 394-9084, (888) 200-9123, hollandmuseum@hollandmuseum.org, www.hollandmuseum.org.
Hours: Mon, Wed-Sat 10am-5pm, Sun 12-5pm. Closed Tue & holidays, extended Tulip Time hours.

Photo: Ted Nielsen

Admission: Museum or houses Adults $7, Seniors $6, Student $4, Family $14. Combination ticket Adults $12, Family $24. *Site Info:* Free street parking. Museum is wheelchair accessible.
The Holland Museum and its satellite historic properties, the Cappon House and the Settlers House, focus on the history, art, industries, and culture of the diverse people who settled in the Holland area. The Holand Museum, located in a 1914 post office, features cultural attractions from the "old country," including Dutch paintings and decorative arts and exhibits from the Netherlands Pavilion of the 1939 New York World's Fair. Local history including Lake Michigan maritime, shipwrecks and resorts; agriculture and manufacturing; service to the community; religious foundations of the "Holland Kolonie"; and an illustrated timeline of area history including its increasing ethnic diversity. Dutch art galleries show growing collection of 17th to 19th century paintings and decorative arts.

Cappon House Museum
Location: 228 W. 9th St.
Contact: (616) 392-6470. *Hours:* May-Dec 12-4pm. Closed Jan-May, extended Tulip Time hours.
The Italianate Cappon House was built by Holland's first mayor and tannery owner Isaac Cappon after the fire of 1871. Used by his

family until the 1980s, the home is now restored and furnished with Grand Rapids furniture.

Settlers House Museum
Location: Settlers House 190 W. 9th St.
Contact: (616) 392-6470. *Hours:* May-Dec 12-4pm. Closed Jan-May, extended Tulip Time hours.
The Settlers House was built by an Irish-Canadian shipbuilder, Thomas Morrissey, in 1867 and was one of the few buildings to survive the Holland Fire. This home highlights locally used period furnishings and hardships faced during the settlement period. Tours begin in Cappon barn.

Joint Archives of Holland
Location: Theil Research Center, 9 E. 10th St., Holland, MI 49423.
Contact: (616) 395-7798, archives@hope.edu,
www.hope.edu/jointarchives. *Mail:* Hope College, P.O. Box 9000.
Hours: 8am-12pm and 1-5pm. *Admission:* Free. *Site Info:* Street parking. Wheelchair accessible.
Hope College and Western Theological Seminary records are housed here. Contents include Reformed Church records including missionary activities and Midwest congregations, 19th Century Dutch immigration to the Midwest, West Michigan history, maritime history, and the pleasure craft industry. The archives also hosts the Pere Marquette Historical Society collection.

Olive Township Museum
Location: 11768 Polk Street, Holland, MI 49424.
Contact: (616) 875-8036, kitkarsten@hotmail.com,
www.olivetownship.com/OTHS. *Hours:* By appointment.
Admission: Donations accepted. *Site Info:* On-site parking. Wheelchair accesssible. Guides available by request. *Events:* Old Settlers Picnic, Christmas Home Tour.
The Olive Township Historical Society, organized in 2004, operates this museum in the former township hall and the Olive Center School providing educational programs and tours of historical sites. Exhibits highlight local and regional artifacts including pioneer schools, a military display, and a church room.

Holly

Hadley House Museum
Location: 06 S. Saginaw Street, Holly, MI 48442.
Contact: (248) 634-9233, hollyhistoricalsoc@comcast.net,
www.hsmichigan.org/holly. *Hours:* Sun 12-4pm in summer, Sun 1-4 in Dec, also by appointment. *Admission:* Adults $2. *Site Info:* Limited parking. Not wheelchair accessible. Self-guided. *Events:* Carry Nation Festival (Aug), Dickens Olde Fashioned Christmas Festival (Dec).
The Holly Historical Society was organized in 1965 and acquired the 1873 Italianate Hadley House in 1986. The home has original interior with period furniture and features historical displays.

Homer

Blair Historical Farm
Location: 26445 M-60 East, Homer, MI 49245.
Contact: (517) 568-3116, joanne.miller43@gmail.com,
www.homerhistoricalsociety.org. *Mail:* 505 Grandview. *Hours:* By
appointment and for special events. *Admission:* Free. *Site Info:* On-site
parking. Partially wheelchair accessible. Docents available. *Events:* Fall
Festival at the Farm (Sep), Car Show (Jul), Herb Workshop (Feb).
The Homer Historical Society was organized 1974 and was given the
farm of George Blair, the first doctor in Homer. Site includes a
farmhouse, barn, sawmill, the old Albion Township Hall, and the Grover
railroad station.

Howell

Howell Depot Museum
Location: 128 Wetmore St.,
Howell, MI 48844.
Contact: (517) 548-6876,
jeboegler@sbcglobal.net,
www.howellareahistorical
society.org. *Mail:* P.O. Box 154.
Hours: May 1st-Oct 31st Sun 9am-
3pm, also by appointment.

Admission: Donation requested. *Site Info:* Free parking. Wheelchair
accessible. *Events:* Howell History Days (May), Melon Festival (Aug),
Legend of Sleepy Howell (Oct).
The Howell Area Historical Society restored and preserves the 1886 Ann
Arbor railroad depot as a fine example of a commercial building from a
period in the community's history and there presents a museum of
interpretive exhibits depicting life in the Howell area. Exhibits include
historical artifacts dating back to the 1860s.

Hudson

William G. Thomson House Museum and Gardens
Location: 101 Summit St., Hudson, MI 49427.
Contact: (517) 448-8125, rlennard@thompsonmuseum.org,
www.thompsonmuseum.org. *Hours:* Mon & Wed 12:45-3:30pm, also by
appointment. *Admission:* Adults $7.50, Seniors $5, Students $3.
Site Info: Street parking. Wheelchair ramp, lift to 2nd floor. Guided tours.
Events: Rummage Sale/Craft Show (Aug).
This 1890s Queen Anne style home is filled with extensive collections
gathered by 3 generations of the Thompson family. Site includes formal
gardens, Oriental antiques, porcelain, and furniture from various periods.

Imlay City

Imlay City Historical Museum
Location: 77 Main Street, Imlay City, MI 48444.
Contact: (810) 724-1111, bswihart1904@charter.net,
www.imlaycityhistoricalmuseum.org/index.htm. *Hours:* Mar-Dec Wed
9:30am-12pm, Sat 1-4pm. *Admission:* Donations accepted. *Site Info:* Free
city parking. Wheelchair accessible. Self-guided. *Events:* Blueberry
Festival (Aug).
Administered by the Imlay City Historical Comission, Inc., the museum
opened 1978 in the historic Grand Trunk depot. Displays in the caboose
and bunk car highlight the military, farm tools, a country doctor's
operating room, photos of Imlay City, and racecar driver Bob Burman.

Ionia

Ionia County Museum
Location: Blanchard House,
251 E. Main St., Ionia, MI
48846.
Contact: (616) 527-6281,
info@ioniahistory.org,
www.ioniahistory.org.
Mail: P.O. Box 1776.
Hours: Jun-Aug & Dec Sun 1-
4 pm, also by appointment.

Admission: $3 suggested donation. *Site Info:* On-site or street parking.
Partially wheelchair accessible: grounds and carriage house, not home.
Guides available.
The Ionia County Historical Society organized in 1974 to secure and
preserve "La Palistina," the 1880 Italianate home of John C. Blanchard, to
preserve local history, and to communicate state and local history. The
upper three levels are restored and furnished with period pieces. The local
history museum on the lower level depicts the early years of Ionia's
settlement and growth with artifacts of daily life in past generations and
displays of "Ionia In Uniform" and "Ionia Business and Industry." A 19th
century carriage house contains displays and is open to tours.

Jenison

Jenison Historical Museum
Location: 28 Port Sheldon Rd. Jenison, MI 49428.
Contact: (616) 457-4398, ltimmer@grcc.edu, www.gtwp.com/history.
Mail: P.O. Box 664. *Hours:* See website for scheduled open houses.
The Tiffany House was built in 1902 for Margaret Husband, a bookkeeper
for the Jenison twins, Lucius and Luman. Furnished with items from this
time period, its displays include medical instruments, a working 5' cash

register from the L&L Store and a Morning Glory Talking Machine. Open houses are held in Jan, Mar, Apr, May, Jul, Sep, Oct, Dec, each with a selected theme.

Kalamazoo

Kalamazoo Valley Museum
Location: 230 N. Rose St., Kalamazoo, MI 49003.
Contact: (800) 772-3370, museumstaff@kvcc.edu, www.kalamazoomuseum.org. *Mail:* P. O. Box 4070. *Hours:* Mon-Sat 9am-5pm, Sun and Holidays 1-5pm. Oct-May Fri 9am-9pm. Closed Easter, Thanksgiving, Christmas Eve, Christmas Day. *Admission:* Free. *Site Info:* Metered street parking or parking ramp ($1.20/hr). Wheelchair accessible. Self-guided. *Events:* Fretboard Festival (March), Festival of Health (March), Safe Halloween (Oct), School Break Hands-On programs.
The museum features exhibits on science, technology, and the history of southwest Michigan. Attractions include an interactive Science Gallery, new History Gallery, Planetarium, Challenger Learning Center, Children's Landscape preschool area, and national traveling exhibits.

Kaleva

Kaleva Bottle House Museum
Location: 14551 Wuoksi St., Kaleva, MI 49645.
Contact: (231) 362-2080, caasiala@jackpine.com, www.kalevami.com/hist_society.html. *Mail:* P.O. Box 252.
Hours: Memorial Day to Labor Day Sat-Sun 12-4pm, Sep-Oct Sat 12-4pm. Also by appointment. *Admission:* $3. *Site Info:* Free street parking. Not wheelchair accessible. Guided tours by appointment.
Events: Juhannus/Mid-Summer Celebration (June), Bake Sale and 5k Walk/Run at Kaleva Days (Jul), Christmas Open House (Dec).
The Kaleva Historical Society, Inc. exists to preserve the history of Kaleva, settled by Finnish immigrants in 1900, and to store and display data and materials so they are available to the community. The Society maintains the historic "Bottle House" built by John Makinen in 1942 of 60,000 soda pop bottles from his bottle factory. Interior historic displays include Ancestors' Pillowcase, Makinen tackle collection, Cooperative Movement Finns, and military.

Kalkaska

Kalkaska County Museum
Location: 335 S. Cedar., Kalkaska, MI 49646.
Contact: (231) 258-9719, www.kalkaskacounty.net/kalk history.asp. *Mail:* P.O. Box 1178. *Hours:* Jun-Aug Wed-Sat 1-4pm, also by appointment. *Admission:* Free. *Site Info:* Parking available. Wheelchair accessible. Self-guided.

This museum opened in 1970 in a former 1911 Grand Rapids and Indiana railroad depot. Artifacts on display concern local history including an 1898 Elmer, an auto built in Kalkaska by Elmer F. Johnson.

Lake Ann

Almira Museum
Location: 19440 Maple St., Lake Ann, MI 49650.
Contact: (231) 275-7362. *Mail:* P.O. Box 91. *Hours:* May-Oct Tue & Sat 1-4pm, winter by appointment. *Admission:* Free. *Site Info:* Free parking. Wheelchair accessible. *Events:* Lake Ann Homecoming (1st Sat Jul). The Almira Historical Society was formed in 1992 and administers a museum containing over 1,300 artifacts and a home with 1940s décor.

Firebarn Museum
The Firebarn has a firetruck and other displays and artifacts including farm equipment.

Lake City

Missaukee County Museum
Location: Missaukee County Park, The Old Bath House, 6201 W. Park., Lake City, MI 49651.
Contact: (231) 839-4963, funnestnan@hotmail.com. *Mail:* P.O. Box 93. *Hours:* Memorial Day to Labor Day Fri-Sun 2-5pm. *Admission:* $2 fee to enter park, Historical Society admission by donation. *Site Info:* Free parking with park admission. Wheelchair accessible. Free guide available. The museum is located in The Old Bath House, built by the Civilian Conservation Corps in the 1930s. Displays focus on the military, agriculture, and logging.

Lansing

Library of Michigan
Location: Michigan Library and Historical Center, 702 W. Kalamazoo, Lansing, MI 48915-1609.
Contact: (517) 373-1580, librarian@michigan.gov, www.michigan.gov/libraryofmichigan. *Hours:* Mon & Thurs 1-6pm, Tue-Wed & Fri 8am-6pm, Sat 9am-5pm. *Admission:* Free. *Site Info:* On-site parking fee charged hourly. Wheelchair accessible. Self-guided. Includes the State Library and State Law Library with services for the blind and physically handicapped. The Martha Griffiths Michigan Rare Book Room contains the most unique or unusual materials held by the Library of Michigan including books, documents, maps, and prints. While the emphasis of the collection is Michigan in general, it does specialize in such subject areas as natural history, law, travel/exploration, fishing, and Native Americans.

Michigan Historical Center

Location: Michigan Library and Historical Center, 702 W. Kalamazoo, Lansing, MI 48915-1609.
Contact: (517) 373-1408, www.michiganhistory.org. *Hours:* Mon-Fri 9am-4:30pm, Sat 10am-4pm, Sun 1-5pm. Archives hours Mon & Thurs 9am-1pm and Mon Wed Fri 1-5pm. *Admission:* Free. *Site Info:* On-site parking fee charged hourly. Wheelchair accessible.
The flagship of the Michigan Historical Museum system, the Michigan Historical Museum celebrates Michigan's rich past from the time of the state's earliest peoples to the late 20th century. The Archives of Michigan is also located at the Center.

Michigan Women's Historical Center and Hall of Fame

Location: 213 W. Main St., Lansing, MI 48933.
Contact: (517) 484-1880, ssoifer@michiganwomen.org, www.michiganwomenshalloffame.org. *Hours:* Museum Wed-Sat 12-4pm, Sun 2-4pm. Business hours Mon-Fri 9am-5pm. *Admission:* Adults $2.50, Seniors $2, Students 5-18 yrs $1. *Site Info:* Free parking. Wheelchair accessible. *Events:* Women's History Month (Mar), Annual Picnic on the Lawn (Jun), Annual Induction Dinner (Oct).
The Michigan Women's Historical Center—the only museum in the state dedicated to women—presents changing exhibits on women's history and art and is the home of the Michigan Women's Hall of Fame, celebrating the achievements of more than 250 women past and present. Located in the historic Cooley-Haze House just blocks from the capitol, the Historical Center is also a favorite of gardening enthusiasts who enjoy the surrounding Cooley Gardens.

R.E. Olds Transportation Museum

Location: 240 Museum Dr., Lansing, MI 48933.
Contact: (517) 372-0422, autos@reoldsmuseum.org, www.reoldsmuseum.org, *Hours:* Tue-Sat 10am-5pm, also Sun 12-5pm in Apr-Oct. Closed holidays. *Admission:* Adults $5, Seniors/Students $3, Families $10, Group Tours $3/person (groups of 15+). *Site Info:* Free parking. Wheelchair accessible. *Events:* Car Capital Celebration (Aug).
Presents the history of the automobile industry in the Lansing area. Exhibits change every 3 months. 50+ vehicles on display with industry memorabilia. An archival collection is located at the museum.

Turner-Dodge House

Location: 100 E. North St., Lansing, MI 48906.
Contact: (517) 483-4220, turnerdodge@ci.lansing.mi.us, www.parks.cityoflansingmi.com/tdodge. *Hours:* Tue-Fri 10am-5pm.
Admission: Lansing residents $3.50, Non-residents $5, Children $2. *Site Info:* Free parking.
Partially wheelchair accessible: first floor only. Guided tours $5/person (groups of 10+). *Events:* Camps throughout the year, Special Teas for children & adults, see website info.

This beautiful location offers a variety of entertainments for all family members. The Classical Revival home was built in 1858 by Marion and James Turner and enlarged in 1903 by daughter Abby and her husband, Frank Dodge. It was the home of Michigan pioneers who helped develop the Capitol City and the state, now restored as a heritage center in Lansing's Old Town. Hosts special exhibits four times each year (see website).

Lapeer

Lapeer Museum
Location: 518 W. Nepessing St., Lapeer, MI 48446.
Contact: (810) 245-5808, lapeerhistoricalmuseum@homestead.com.
Mail: P.O. Box 72, Lapeer, MI 48446. *Hours:* Wed & Sat 10am-3pm.
Admission: Donations accepted. *Site Info:* Nearby parking. Courthouse and Farm Shop are wheelchair accessible, Museum is not. Guides available upon request. *Events:* Farm Fest (Aug), Concert of Historic Music (Nov).
The Lapeer County Historical Society was established in 1969 to preserve county history and to present it to the public. This museum houses exhibits pertaining to Lapeer County and the lives of its residents.

1846 Courthouse
Location: W. Nepessing St. and N. Court St.
Hours: Open Sat May-Oct.
The oldest continuously used courthouse in Michigan. Exhibits focus on its history and role in the community.

Davis Brothers Farm Shop Museum
Location: 3520 Davis Lake Rd.
Hours: By appointment.
A museum with displays of farm life in Lapeer.

Leeland

Leelanau Historical Museum
Location: 203 E. Cedar St., Leland, MI 49654.
Contact: (231) 256-7475, info@leelanauhistory.org,
www.leelanauhistory.org. *Mail:* P.O. Box 246. *Hours:* Wed-Fri 10am-4pm, Sat 10am-3pm. *Admission:* By donation. *Site Info:* Free on-site parking. Wheelchair accessible. Self-guided. *Events:* North Manitou Island Day Trip (Aug), Boats on the Wall (Sep).
The Leelanau Historical Society inspires people to explore the past, understand the present, and envision the future of the diverse cultures in the Leelanau Peninsula and its islands. Featuring a shipwreck exhibit and the Loss and Legacy Anishinabeck Arts Collection (baskets and quillwork from the Leelanau Peninsula's Odawa artists).

Lexington

Sanilac County Historic Village and Museum
Location: 228 S. Ridge St., Lexington, MI 48450.
Contact: (810) 622-9946, sanilacmuseum@gmail.com,
www.sanilaccountymuseum.org. *Mail:* 3043 Lakeshore. *Hours:* Summer
Wed-Fri 12-4pm, also by appointment. *Admission:* $5. *Site Info:* Limited
wheelchair accessibility. Guide available. *Events:* Log Cabin Days, Civil
War Days, Hobo Day (at the Depot).
The Historic Village, on the 1853 estate of Dr. Joseph Loop, has twelve
historic buildings. The country doctor's 20-room Victorian mansion is the
flagship of village that includes Platt's General Store circa 1900, the 1843
Huckins one-room schoolhouse, 1883 Banner pioneer log cabin, and a
historic barn theater. Permanent exhibits include a marine shipwreck room
and separate dairy industry museum, along with old-time carriages,
military, and Native American exhibits.

Lincoln Park

Lincoln Park Historical Museum
Location: 1335 Southfield Rd., Lincoln Park, MI 48146.
Contact: (313) 386-3137, lpmuseum@gmail.com, www.lphistorical.org.
Hours: Tue-Thurs 1-5pm. *Admission:* Free. *Site Info:* On-site parking.
Wheelchair accessible. Guides available upon request, groups by
appointment. *Events:* Memorial Bell Ringing, Veterans Recognition Day,
Holiday Open House.
The Lincoln Park Historical Society was organized in 1954 and collects
artifacts of Lincoln Park's founding era, from the early settlers to the
present. Displays include artifacts from farms, kitchens, a gun exhibit, a
camera exhibit, and a music room. Rotating special exhibits are also
displayed.

Lowell

Lowell Area Historical Museum
Location: 325 W. Main St.,
Lowell, MI 49331.
Contact: (616) 897-7688,
history@lowellmuseum.org,
www.lowellmuseum.org.
Mail: P.O. Box 81.
Hours: Tue & Sat-Sun 1-4pm,
Thurs 1-8pm. *Admission:*
Adults $3, Children (5-17) $1.50, under 5 free. *Site Info:* On-site parking.
Wheelchair accessible. Docents available, tours by appointment.
The museum opened in 2001 in 1873 residential duplex, the Graham

Building, listed in the National Register of Historic Places. Exhibits highlight early Lowell history, business, industry, and the Lowell Showboat.

Ludington

Historic White Pine Village
Location: 1687 S. Lakeshore Dr., Ludington, MI 49431.
Contact: (231) 843-4808, info@historicwhitepinevillage.org, www.historicwhitepinevillage.org. *Hours:* May-Oct Tue-Sat 10am-5pm. Memorial Day to Labor Day Sun 1-5pm. *Admission:* Adults $9, Children 6-17 $6. *Site Info:* Street parking. Partially wheelchair accessible. Self-guided. *Events:* Down on the Farm (Aug), Logging Days (Sep), Autumn Days (Oct).
Historic White Pine Village opened in 1976 and contains twenty-nine buildings including a one-room schoolhouse, lumbering museum, blacksmith shop, fire hall, general store, trapper's cabin, sawmill, doctor's office, chapel, courthouse, print shop, maritime museum, post office, sugar house, hardware store, farmstead, cooper's shop, car museum, town hall with old-fashioned ice cream parlor, the Rose Hawley Museum, and the Mason County Sports Hall of Fame.

Mackinaw City

Mackinac State Historic Parks
Location: See below.
Contact: (231) 436-4100, mackinacparks@michigan.gov, www.mackinacparks.com. *Mail:* P.O. Box 873, Mackinaw City, MI 49701. *Site Info:* On-site parking adjacent to Visitor's Center. Partially wheelchair accessible (see "Guide to Access" brochure at sites). Costumed interpretive guides daily.

Colonial Michilimackinac
Location: 102 W. Straits Ave., Mackinaw City, MI 49701
Hours: Early May to mid-Oct 9am-4pm (peak summer season hours extended to 6pm). *Admission:* Adults $10.50, Youth (5-17) $6.50, includes all Mackinac Island sites, combination tickets and family passes available.
This French fur-trading village and military outpost was founded in 1715, later occupied by the British who abandoned it in 1780 to establish a new fort on Mackinac Island. The reconstructed fortified village of 13 buildings is as it appeared 1770s. Redcoats, traders, and colonial ladies demonstrate military activities and domestic arts of the time. Accessed through the Visitor's Center under the south approach to the Mackinac Bridge.

Historic Mill Creek Discovery Park
Location: 9001 US-23, Southeast of Mackinaw City.
Hours: Early May to mid-Oct 9am-4pm (peak summer season hours extended to 5pm). *Admission:* Adults $8, Youth (5-17) $4.75, Combination tickets and family passes available.

As the Straits' first industrial complex, this site provided lumber for settlement of Mackinac Island in the 1790s. Demonstrations are given of both hand-saw techniques and the reconstructed 18th century water-driven sawmill. The site also features natural history programs, nature trails, and daily "high ropes" adventure tours.

Old Mackinac Point Lighthouse
Location: 526 North Huron Ave.
Hours: Early May to mid-Oct 9am-4pm (Peak summer season, hours extended to 5pm). *Admission:* Adults $6, Youth (5-17) $4, Combination tickets and family passes available.

Erected in 1892, this lighthouse served more than 60 years and has been restored to its 1910 appearance with first-floor period settings and hands-on exhibits. Interpreters lead frequent tours up the tower and its lantern room.

Mackinaw Area Historic Village
Location: 501 Wilderness Park Dr., Mackinaw City, MI 49701.
Contact: (231) 436-4006, mail@mackinawhistory.org, www.mackinawhistory.org. *Mail:* P.O. Box 999. *Hours:* See website for current hours. *Admission:* Free. *Site Info:* On-site parking. Partially wheelchair accessible. Free guide available by appointment.
Events: Summer Celebration (Aug).

The Mackinaw Area Historical Society was organized in 1996 to collect and share the history of Mackinaw City, Bliss, and Levering as well as the townships of Wawatam, Mackinaw, and Carp Lake. The Historic Village in Mackinaw City includes a pest house, ice house, storage building, school, church, privy, maple sugar shack, lumber mill, clothes pin factory (lath mill), depot, and pavilion.

Manchester

John Schneider Blacksmith Shop Museum
Location: 324 E. Main St., Manchester, MI 48158.
Contact: (734) 428-0159, mahs-info@manchesterarea historicalsociety.org, www.manchesterareahistorical society.org. *Mail:* P.O. Box 56.
Hours: Call or see website.
Events: Christmas Eve Luminaria.
The Manchester Area Historical Society promotes the appreciation of history and operates the museum for educational purposes.

Manistee

S.S. City of Milwaukee
Location: 99 Arthur St., Manistee, MI 49660.
Contact: lspencer@carferry.com, www.carferry.com. *Mail:* P.O. Box
394. *Hours:* Full tours leave at 11am, 12:30pm, 2pm, 3:30pm and 5pm.
Half-hour tours leave on the half-hour. Apr Sat-Sun 11am-3pm, last tour
leaves at 2pm. May Fri-Sun 11am-5pm, last tour leaves at 4pm. Jun-Aug
Thurs-Mon 11am-6pm, last tour leaves at 5pm. Sep Fri-Sun.
Admission: Full tour (1 hr) Adults $8, Seniors & Children (ages 6 - 17)
$5, Family Rate (4 or more) $25. 30 min. tour Adults $5 Seniors &
Children (ages 6-17) $4. Members & Children under 6 free for both tours.
The S.S. City of Milwaukee collects, archives, and exhibits material of
historical and educational significance pertaining to the legacy of the
Great Lakes railroad car ferries.

Marine City

Marine City Pride and Heritage Museum
Location: 405 S. Main St.,
Marine City, MI 48039.
Contact: (810) 765-5446,
marinecitymuseum@hotmail.com,
www.marinecitymuseum.org.
Mail: P.O. Box 184. *Hours:* Jun-
Oct Sat-Sun 1-4pm. *Admission:*
Donations accepted. *Site Info:* Free
parking. Wheelchair accessible. Free guides available, tours by
appointment. *Events:* East China Community Band concerts in Broadway
Park.
Originally built in 1847 by Eber Brock Ward to house the Newport
Academy, run by his sister Emily Ward. Artifacts and archival collections
are featured in three galleries: lifestyle with furnished rooms dating back
to the 1800s, business, commercial and maritime including a 4 1/2 by 36-
foot diorama of the Belle River in 1885, when 5 shipyards were engaged
in producing Great Lakes ships. A blacksmith shop is located on museum
grounds.

Marshall

Honolulu House
Location: 107 N. Kalamazoo, Marshall, MI 49068.
Contact: (269) 781-8544, mhsdirector@mac.com,
www.marshallhistoricalsociety.org. *Hours:* Daily May-Sep 12-5pm, Oct
Thurs-Sun 12-5 pm. *Admission:* Adults $5, Seniors & Students 12-18 $4,
Children 12 & under free with paid adult. *Site Info:* Free parking.
Wheelchair accessible. Guided tours available. *Events:* Historic Home
Tour (Sep), Christmas Candlelight Walk (Dec).

The home of the Marshall Historical Society, this unique structure was built in 1860 as a private residence for Judge Abner Pratt upon his return from the Sandwich (Hawaiian) Islands where he served as U.S. Consul. House and is said to resemble the executive mansion he occupied while serving in Honolulu from 1857-1859. A blend of Italianate, Gothic Revival and Polynesian influences, the house is built of Marshall sandstone faced with vertical boards and battens. Wall and ceiling paintings, carpets, and furniture have all been restored to recreate its 1880s splendor.

Capitol Hill School
Built in 1860, Capitol Hill School survives on land adjacent to the area intended as the site for Michigan's state capitol. The two-room schoolhouse served the city for 101 years and is used as a museum where children and teachers are encouraged to relive an 1800s school day.

G.A.R. Hall
Built in 1902 by the Grand Army of the Republic as a meeting place for the veterans of the Civil War and their sons, this structure is now the Marshall Historical Society's Archival Center and Military Museum. Collection includes artifacts from the Civil War, the Spanish-American War, World War I, and World War II along with other Marshall memorabilia.

Mason

Mason Area Historical Museum
Location: Corner of Barnes St. and W. Oak St., Mason, MI 48854.
Contact: (517) 697-9837, www.masonmuseum.com.
Mail: P.O. Box 44. *Hours:* Tue-Thurs Sat 1-3pm.
Admission: Free. *Site Info:* Street parking. Museum is wheelchair accessible, Pink School is not. Free guide available. *Events:* Tours of Pink School by apointment at 707 W. Ash St. Antique Show and Sale (Feb), Pie Sale fundraisers, Victorian Garden Social (Jul).

The museum, administered by the Mason Area Historical Society, seeks to preserve and educate people about the history of Mason. Exhibits include artifacts related to its industries and institutions.

Mears

Oceana Historical Park and Museum
Location: Fox Rd. 2 blocks west of downtown Mears, MI.
Contact: (231) 873-2600, info@oceanahistory.org, www.oceanahistory.org. *Mail:* 114 Dryden St, Hart, MI 49420.
Hours: Weekends Jun-Aug 1-4pm. *Admission:* Free. *Site Info:*On-site parking. Partially wheelchair accessible. Docent available.
Events: Postcard Show (Jun), Pleasant Afternoon (Aug).
The former home of Swift Lathers, editor and publisher of the Mears Newz from 1914 until his death in 1970, was given to the Society for a

museum in Mears on land now known as the Oceana Historical Park. In 1985, the society received the Swedish Mission Church in Mears which was moved to the museum park in 2007. In 1998, the Transportation Museum was built on the park grounds providing space for storage of artifacts, meetings, and a showroom for automotive exhibits. In 2008, the society purchased the original town hall in Mears, now being used as exhibit hall. Robinson Building displays include exhibits on Oceana County History. The Transportation Museum holds changing exhibits of antique cars, trucks, dune buggies, and related memorabilia. The Old Town Hall displays changing special exhibits.

Mesick

Marilla Museum and Pioneer Place

Location: 9991 Marilla Rd., Mesick, MI 49668.
Contact: (231) 378-2123, boja@kaltelnet.net, www.allartmanistee.com.
Mail: 22296 Benton Rd.
Hours: May-Oct Sat 2-5pm, also by appointment.
Admission: Donations accepted. *Site Info:* On-site parking. Partially wheelchair accessible: 1st floor of Museum and Pioneer Houses only. Docent on site. *Events:* Strawberry Social, Pioneer Christmas. View webpage for current programs and events.

Two rooms in the lower level of the former 1920 New Consolidated School in Marilla Township are available for viewing. The grounds contain a 1900 mortise and tenon wagon-style barn with agricultural and logging displays, an 1870 two story log house that served as a way station for the overland stage, and a replica log cabin furnished to show the life of Swedish immigrant logger and trapper.

Midland

Alden B. Dow Home and Studio

Location: 315 Post St., Midland, MI 48640.
Contact: (989) 839-2744, info@abdow.org, www.abdow.org.
Hours: Tours Feb-Dec Mon-Sat at 2pm, Fri-Sat at 10am.
Admission: Adults $12, Students (ages 8+) $7. *Site Info:* Nearby parking. Not wheelchair accessible. All tours guided (bus groups welcome with reservation). *Events:* Autumn Reflections Tours (Oct, call for reservation), other special programming throughout the year.

Alden B. Dow was an organic architect. His home and studio is a National Historic Landmark open for tours and educational programming. Original furnishings, ceramic and glass collection from the 1930s-1960s, personal and professional libraries.

Post Street Archives

Location: 1018 W. Main St., Midland, MI 48640-4264.
Contact: (989) 832-0870. *Hours:* Mon-Fri 8am-12pm. *Admission:* Free.
Site Info: Free parking.
The Post Street Archives, a division of the Herbert H. and Grace A. Dow
Foundation, collects, maintains, and makes accessible historical materials
concerning the family of Herbert H. Dow and Grace A. Dow. The
archives has over 800 linear feet of records, including personal papers,
publications, newspaper collections, books, films, maps, audio recordings,
slides, videotapes, memorabilia, oral histories, and an extensive
photograph collection.

Dow Gardens

Location: 1809 Eastman Ave., Midland, MI 48640.
Contact: (989) 631-2677, mcguire@dowgardens.org,
www.dowgardens.org. *Mail:* 1018 W. Main St. *Hours:* Jan-Apr 14 9am-
4pm, Apr 15-Sep 6 9am-8:30pm, Sep 7-Oct 31 9am-6:30pm, Nov 1-Dec
31 9am-4:15. *Admission:* Adults $5, Youth (6-17) $1. *Site Info:* Free
parking. Wheelchair accessible (wheelchairs or amigos available for
rental). Group tours $2/person (5+ people). *Events:* Tours of Herbert H.
and Grace A. Dow home, Fri 1:30 (Summer Mon-Fri 2pm), $7/person,
reservations required.
Dow Gardens was started in 1899 by Herbert Dow, founder of Dow
Chemical Company, on 8 acres of land with work continuted by his son,
architect Alden Dow. Today the Gardens, expanded to 110 acres, feature
some of the finest seasonal horticultural displays in the Midwest. Check
website for current activities, including Art in the Gardens and musical
events.

Heritage Park

Location: 3417 W. Main St., Midland, MI 48640.
Contact: (989) 631-5930, skory@mcfta.org, swinson@mcfta.org,
www.mcfta.org. *Hours:* Wed-Sat 10am-5pm, Sun 1-5pm.
Admission: Adults $5, Children $3, MCHS Members free. *Site Info:* On-
site parking. Wheelchair accessible. Guided tours available for groups by
appointment (call for cost). *Events:* Mother-Daughter Tea, Victorian
Funeral and Cemetery Tour, Antique Appraisal Event, Bradley Home
Christmas.
Heritage Park operates three main attractions: the Herbert D. Doan
Midland County History Center, the 1874 Bradley Home Museum and
Carriage House, and the Herbert H. Dow Historical Museum. The Doan
History Center offers the Midland History Gallery and hands-on
interactive exhibits. The Bradley Home is one of Michigan's only hands-
on historic house museums with Victorian furnishings, fixtures, and
costumes. The carriage house features fifteen horse-drawn vehicles. The
Dow Museum chronicles the life of the Dow Chemical Co. and explains
the many inventions created in Midland that we use everyday.

Milan

Hack House Museum
Location: 775 County St., Milan, MI 48160.
Contact: (734) 439-4007, alford@sbcglobal.net, www.historicmilan.com.
Mail: P.O. Box 245. *Hours:* May-Nov Fri 1-4pm, also by appointment.
Admission: Adults $2, Youth (5-12) $1. *Site Info:* Free parking. Self-guided.
The Milan Area Historical Society maintains two restored structures: Old Fire Barn (now office and meeting space) and the 1888 Hack House, a Stick-style historic house museum including four outbuildings. Engages in community outreach programs such as public lectures, programs aimed at schoolchildren, and special events.

Milford

Milford Historical Museum
Location: 124 E. Commerce St., Milford, MI 48381.
Contact: (248) 685-7308, milfordhistory@hotmail.com, www.milfordhistory.org. *Hours:* Wed & Sat 1-4pm.
Admission: Donations accepted. *Site Info:* Street parking (metered or free) and 2 hr. parking lot. Partially wheelchair accessible (lower level only).
Events: Granny's Attic Yard Sale (Jul), Homes Tour (Sep).
The Milford Historical Society was organized exclusively for educational purposes. It brings together people who are interested in history, especially the history of the Village of Milford and Milford Township. Attractions include a Victorian-style parlor, children's toy area, dining room, kitchen, bedroom, and an 1832 one-room cabin replica.

Millersburg

D&M Railroad Depot
Location: Main St. and E. Luce St., Millersburg, MI 49759.
Contact: (989) 734-7197. *Mail:* P.O. Box 30. *Hours:* Labor Day Weekend 9am-5pm or call Jeff Whitsitt at (989) 733-8404 for appointment.
Admission: Free. *Site Info:* On-site parking. Docent available.
Founded in 1996, the Millersburg Area Historical Society showcases artifacts from the Millersburg area in the D&M Railroad Depot, the only depot remaining in Presque Isle County.

Montague

Montague Museum
Location: Corner of Church St. and Meade St., Montague, MI 49437.
Contact: (231) 893-3055, cityofmontague@aol.com. *Mail:* 8636 Old Channel Trail. *Hours:* Weekends Memorial Day to Labor Day 1-5pm,

Business Hours 1-5pm. *Admission:* Donations accepted. *Site Info:* On-site parking. Not wheelchair accessible. Guide available by appointment. These displays focus on the lumber era on the White River and White Lake, local farming (tools and pictures), military guns and clothing, Admiral Byrd's South Pole explorations (books, tools, etc.), Montague's 1962 Miss America, Nancy Ann Fleming, local art, photo collections, fire and police equipment, post office, and Indian Room.

Montrose

Montrose Historical and Pioneer Telephone Museum
Location: 144 E. Hickory St., Montrose, MI 48457.
Contact: (810) 639-6644, joe@montrosemuseum.com, www.montrosemuseum.com. *Mail:* P.O. Box 577. *Hours:* Sun 1-5pm, Mon-Tue 9am-3pm. *Admission:* Free. *Site Info:* On-site parking. Wheelchair accessible. Group tours available $2/person, Children free. *Events:* Blueberry Festival (Aug).
Originally the telephone office for the Public Service Telephone Co., this museum contains hands-on, working exhibits of antique telephone equipment and historical highlights of Montrose. Over 400 telephones on display, local history exhibits, and rotating displays on loan from individuals.

Mount Clemens

Crocker House Museum

Location: 15 Union, Mount Clemens, MI 48043.
Contact: (586) 465-2488, crockerhousemuseum@sbc global.net, www.crockerhouse museum.com. *Hours:* Mar-Dec Tue-Thurs 10am-4pm. 1st Sun of month 1-4 pm. Closed holidays.
Admission: Adult $3, Child $1 suggested donation. *Site Info:* Metered lot, free street parking. Not wheelchair accessible. Guided tours. *Events:* Garden Walk (Jun), Cemetery Walk (Oct), Victorian Christmas (Dec).
This 1869 Italianate home housed the first two mayors of Mt. Clemens and provides a late Victorian home-life experience reminiscent of the mineral bath era of Mount Clemens. The museum also includes displays of local and county history. The main floor interprets a home as it would have appeared in the 1870s-80s in Mount Clemens. The upper floor features local history displays.

Michigan Transit Museum
Location: 200 Grand Ave., Mount Clemens, MI 48046. *Contact:* (586) 463-1863, mtm1973@juno.com, www.michigantransitmuseum.org.
Mail: P.O. Box 12. *Hours:* Sat-Sun 1-4pm. *Admission:* Train ticket fare Adults $7, Children 4-12 $3, Children 4 and under free (prices subject to

change for special train excursions, reservations suggested for popular Polar Express ride). *Site Info:* Parking in city lot. Museum wheelchair accessible. *Events:* Polar Express ride (Winter).
At this railroad museum in the 1859 Mount Clemens depot visitors can embark on weekend rail excursions Jun-Sep. Check website for schedule and restrictions.

Mount Pleasant

Museum of Cultural and Natural History
Location: Central Michigan University, 103 Rowe Hall, Mount Pleasant, MI 48859.
Contact: (989) 774-3829, cmuseum@cmich.edu, www.museum.cmich.edu. *Hours:* Mon-Fri 8am-5pm, Sat-Sun 1-5pm.
Admission: Suggested donation Adult $1, Child $0.50. *Site Info:* Metered parking or parking passes available. Wheelchair accessible. Guided tours available by appointment. *Events:* Tour Tuesdays (Jul).
This of Central Michigan University museum is dedicated to the study of zoology, geology, history, anthropology and Native American art. Exhibits include pre-historic glaciers and mastodons, Native Americans and fur traders, Civil War soldiers and lumbermen, and wildlife from bats to walleye.

Clarke Historical Library
Location: Central Michigan University, Mt Pleasant, MI 48859.
Contact: (989) 774-3352, clarke@cmich.edu, www.clarke.cmich.edu.
Hours: Mon-Fri 8am-5pm. *Admission:* Free. *Site Info:* Metered parking. Wheelchair accessible.
Clarke Library is the special collections unit of Central Michigan University Libraries. Its 1,200 sq. ft. exhibit gallery features two exhibits each year, highlighting some aspect of the library's collection.

Muskegon

Muskegon Heritage Museum
Location: 561 W. Western Ave., Muskegon, MI 49440.
Contact: (231) 722-1363, www.muskegonheritage.org. *Hours:* Mid-May to mid-Oct Fri-Sat 11am-4pm, also by appointment. *Admission:* adults $4, children (5-12 yrs) $2, under 5 yrs free. *Site Info:* Street or city lot parking. Wheelchair accessible. Group and special tours by appointment. *Events:* Summer Celebration (Jul).
The Muskegon Heritage Museum focuses on Muskegon's industrial history and the historic homes and buildings in the city. Exhibits include Muskegon's foundries, a working print shop, a Corliss valve steam engine, the Van Voorthuysen Iron Works hand forge and tools, woodworking machinery and tools from 1800s, log marks and logging tools, a paper mill display, a Victorian parlor, and more.

Lakeshore Museum Center

Location: 430 W Clay Ave, Muskegon, MI 49440.
Contact: (231) 722-0278, info@lakeshoremuseum.org, www.lakeshoremuseum.org.
Hours: Mon-Fri 9:30am-4:30pm, Sat-Sun 12-4pm.
Admission: Free. *Site Info:* On-site parking. Wheelchair accessible. Some galleries have video guide components. *Events:* Lumber Barons' Ball (Oct), progressive dinner with silent auction and entertainment, Holiday Tours (Thanksgiving-Dec).

The Museum Center preserves and interprets the natural and cultural history of Muskegon County. Permanent exhibits include "Michigan: from the Depths of Time," "Coming to the Lakes," "Habitat Gallery," and "Body Works." Explore hands-on galleries, lumbering, science, and the human body. The museum administers three additional sites.

Hackley and Hume Historic Site

Location: 484 W. Webster Ave.
Hours: May-Oct Wed-Sun 12-4pm. *Admission:* Adults (13+) $3, Children free. *Site Info:* Street Parking. Houses not wheelchair accessible, City Barn is accessible. Tours are guided.

This site includes the restored residences of Muskegon lumber barons Charles Hackley and Thomas Hume: Queen Anne style homes built in 1880's feature lavish woodcarvings, stenciling, stained glass windows, and period furnishings. Visit the "Under Attack!" display in the barn to examine methods employed by museum curators to protect and preserve artifacts.

Scolnik House of the Depression Era

Location: 504 W. Clay Ave.
Hours: May-Oct Wed-Sun 12-4pm. *Admission:* Free.
Site Info: Street Parking. Not wheelchair accessible. Guides available to provide information for walk-through tours.

This two-story house in 1930s style with furnishings, toys, books, and bric-a-brac of time period is interpreted through the stories of two fictional families living in the era of the Great Depression.

Fire Barn Museum

Location: 510 W. Clay Ave.
Hours: May-Oct Wed-Sun 12-4pm. *Admission:* Free.
Site Info: Street parking. Partially wheelchair accessible (1st floor only). Docents on hand to answer questions.

This site is a replica of Hackley Hose Company No. 2, formed in 1875 after several devastating fires. Heroic firefighting traditions are explored throuh photographs, uniforms, alarm and call box, hose cart, ladders, and a1923 LaFrance Class B Pumper.

New Boston

Samuel Adams Historical Museum
Location: 37236 Huron River Dr., New Boston, MI 48164.
Contact: (734) 753-4220, hurtwphis@yahoo.com. *Mail:* P.O. Box 38.
Hours: Call for hours. *Admission:* Free. *Site Info:* On-site parking.
Wheelchair accessible. Self-guided. *Events:* Memorial Day, Antique
Appraisals, Ice Cream Social, Market Day, Historical Days, Porch Sale,
Halloween, Holiday Open House.
The Huron Township Historical Society administers this 1890 home
furnished and decorated in period style

Northville

Mill Race Village
Location: 215 Griswold St., Northville, MI 48167.
Contact: (248) 348-1845, mrv1845@yahoo.com,
www.millracenorthville.org. *Hours:* Village Mid-Jun to Mid-Oct Sun 1-
4pm, Business Office Mon-Fri 9am-1pm, Archives Thurs-Fri 9am-1pm.
Admission: Free. *Site Info:* Free on-site parking. Partially wheelchair
accessible. Docents available, private tours for groups of 10 or more $3
per person. *Events:* Victorian Teas, Lectures, Independence Day
Activities, Victorian Festival (Sep), Children's Christmas Workshop,
Christmas in the Village, and more.
In 1977, the Northville Historical Society created Mill Race Village to
preserve examples of architectural styles common to Northville pre-1900.
The Village is located on land donated to the city by Ford Motor Co. and
contains 10 relocated or reconstructed buildings including a church,
school, gazebo, blacksmith, interurban station, general store, and four
homes.

Okemos

Meridian Historical Village
Location: 5113 Marsh Rd., Okemos, MI 48805.
Contact: (517) 347-7300,
picketfence@comcast.net, www.merhistvill.org.
Mail: P.O. Box 155. *Hours:* May-Oct Sat 10am-
2pm, also by appointment. *Admission:* Donations
accepted. *Site Info:* Free parking. Partially
wheelchair accessible. Guided tours by
appointment for a small fee.
Events: Victorian Tea (May), Heritage Festival
(Oct), Christmas in the Village (Dec).
The Historical Village, administered by Friends of Historic Meridian, is
located behind the Nokomis Learning Center. The site contains a living
history museum with nine structures and offers a variety of community
outreach and educational programs.

Old Mission

Old Mission Peninsula Historical Society
Location: Lighthouse Park, Old Mission, MI 49673.
Contact: (231) 223-7560, info@omphistoricalsociety.org,
www.omphistoricalsociety.org. *Mail:* P.O. Box 115. *Hours:* Morning to
dusk. *Events:* Log Cabin Day (Jun).
The site contains the 1850s Hessler log house and the homestead of Rev.
Peter Dougherty, who established the peninsula's namesake Indian
mission.

Omena

Putnam-Cloud Tower House
Location: 5045 N. West Bayshore Dr., Omena, MI 49670. *Contact:* (231)
386-7539, ndean@torchlake.com, www.omenahistoricalsociety.com.
Mail: P.O. Box 75. *Hours:* Jun-Oct Sat-Sun 1-4pm, Apr-May & Nov-Dec
Sat 1-4pm. *Admission:* Free. *Site Info:* Street parking. Wheelchair
accessible. Guided tours by appointment.
The Omena Historical Society restored the Putnam-Cloud Tower House
as museum and community gathering place. Information on exhibits and
programs is available on its website.

Orchard Lake

Orchard Lake Museum
Location: 3951 Orchard Lake Rd., Orchard Lake, MI 48325.
Contact: (248) 682-2279, buzz@qlinc.com, www.gwbhs.com. *Mail:* P.O.
Box 253055. *Hours:* 2nd Sun of the month 1-4 pm. Research
opportunities by appointment. *Admission:* Donations accepted.
Site Info: On-site parking. Wheelchair accessible. *Events:* Public tours of
Apple Island (May).
The Greater West Bloomfield Historical Society serves West Bloomfield,
Sylvan Lake, Keego Harbor, and Orchard Lake, operates the museum as a
repository for items of historic value and significance pertaining to West
Bloomfield Township, and is steward of Orchard Lake's Apple Island.
Collection includes images, oral and written histories, manuscripts, and
objects including a wooden dugout and statue of Chief Pontiac.

Oscoda

Yankee Air Force Museum- Wurtsmith Division
Location: 4071 E. Van Ettan, Oscoda, MI 48750.
Contact: (989) 739-7555, (989) 736-7835, yafray@yahoo.com,
www.wurtsmith-yaf-museum.org. *Mail:* P.O. Box 664. *Hours:* May-Oct
Fri-Sun 11am-3pm. Groups also by appointment.

Admission: Adults $5, Youth (under 12) $3. *Site Info:* Free parking. Wheelchair accessible. *Events:* Fly-in/Pancake Breakfast (Jul).
Aviation artifacts date from before the Wright Brothers to the present day, with special emphasis on the military units that were based at Wurtsmith beginning with Camp Skeel in the 1920s. Historic aircraft under restoration include a Cessna O-1A "Bird-Dog", two T-33As, a Bell UH-1H helicopter, a Waco, and a CG-4A troop glider.

Otsego

Otsego Area Historical Museum
Location: 218 N. Farmer, Otsego, MI 49078.
Contact: (269) 692-3775, oahs@otsegohistory.org, www.otsegohistory.org. *Mail:* P.O. Box 424. *Hours:* Wed 5pm-7pm, Sat 10am-2pm and by appointment. *Admission:* Free. *Site Info:* Free parking. Wheelchair accessible.
The Otsego Area Historical Society illustrates the unique history of the Otsego area through exhibits, displays, and educational programs highlighting the pioneer history of Michigan and the papermaking industry of Otsego's seven operational mills.

Ovid

Ovid Historical Society Museum
Location: 131 East Williams Rd., Ovid, MI 48866.
Contact: (989) 834-5517, ovidhs67@yahoo.com. *Mail:* P.O. Box 4.
Hours: Historical Room Wed 3-8pm, Sat 10am-1pm. Museum 2nd & 4th Sundays 2-4pm. *Admission:* Free.
The Ovid Historical Society, organized in 1992, maintains a historical house filled with antiques and a historical room with artifacts and documents related to Ovid history and people.

Owosso

Shiawassee County Museum
Location: 1997 N. M-52, Owosso, MI 48867.
Contact: (989) 723-2371, arch@shianet.org, www.shiawassee countyhistsoc.org. *Mail:* P.O. Box 526. *Hours:* May-Sep Sat-Sun 1-4pm.
Admission: By donation. *Site Info:* On-site parking. Wheelchair accessible. Docent available.
Preserving the past for future generations, the museum has primitive artifacts and professional, technical, and agricultural items from the 19th century to present.

Oxford

Northeast Oakland Historical Society
Location: 1 N. Washington St., Oxford, MI 48371.
Contact: (248) 628-8413, www.orion.lib.mi.us/nohs. *Hours:* Sat 1-4pm,
Wed 1-4pm Jun-Aug only, also by appointment. *Admission:* Free.
Site Info: Free parking. Self-guided, group tours by appointment.
Events: Elementary School Tours, Oxford Days (Aug).
Located in the in former Oxford Savings Bank, this museum hosts
changing exhibits plus the Around-the-World Doll Collection, local
furniture, a tin shop display, and other local artifacts.

Pentwater

Pentwater Historical Museum
Location: 327 N. Hancock St., Pentwater, MI 49449.
Contact: (231) 869-5820, info@pentwaterhistoricalsociety.org,
www.pentwaterhistoricalsociety.org. *Mail:* P.O. Box 54. *Hours:* Mid-Jun
to mid-Sep Mon, Thurs, & Sat 2-5pm. *Admission:* Free.
Site Info: Wheelchair accessible. Self-guided.
The museum, located on the lower level of the Pentwater Township
building, contains exhibits highlighting logging, shipping, and industry.
The Society has also identified historic buildings and installed interpretive
signs. Tour maps of the village are available.

Plymouth

Plymouth Historical Museum
Location: 155 S. Main St. Plymouth, MI 48170.
Contact: (734) 455-8940, director@plymouthhistory.org,
www.plymouthhistory.org. *Hours:* Wed, Fri, Sat-Sun 1-4pm. Office hours
Mon, Wed, 9:30am-5pm. *Admission:* Adult $5, Child 6-17 $2, Family
$10. *Site Info:* Free parking. Wheelchair accessible. Self-guided.
The museum, owned by the Plymouth Historical Society, focuses on
Plymouth history, Daisy Air Rifles, the Atter Motor Car Co., Civil War
history (especially the 24th Michigan Regiment), and the Petz Lincoln
Collection.

Pointe Aux Pins

Bois Blanc Island Museum
Location: Bob-Lo Dr. west of Hawk's Landing, Pointe Aux Pins, MI
49775.
Contact: (231) 634-7025, hutchtwo@hughes.net. *Mail:* P.O. Box 933.
Hours: Jul-Labor Day Tue, Thurs, & Sat 10am-2pm.
Admission: Donations accepted. *Site Info:* On-site parking. Partially
wheelchair accessible (small step at side entrance). Guides available.

Events: Bake sale at Island Fun Day, ice cream social (Jul), Informational Lectures, Memory Nights (Aug).

The museum, administered by the Bois Blanc Island Historical Society, shares a building with the library. Its collection includes lumber industry tools, relics from the soldiers on Mackinac Island who used Bois Blanc Island as a woodlot, household items, books from the island school, and cassette tapes of oral history.

Pontiac

Pine Grove Museum/Governor Moses Wisner Home
Location: 405 Cesar E. Chavez, Pontiac, MI 48342.
Contact: (248) 338-6732, office@ocphs.org, www.ocphs.org. *Hours:* By appointment. *Admission:* Adults $5, Children (age 12 and under) $3.
Site Info: On-site parking. Partially wheelchair accessible. Guides dressed in period costumes available with advance notice for groups of five or more. *Events:* Summer Social, Victorian Open House, see website for dates and times.

"Pine Grove," the estate of Michigan's 12th governor and Civil War patriot, Moses Wisner, is administered by the oldest county-based historical society in Michigan: the Oakland County Pioneer Historical Society. The grounds include a Greek Revival Home (c. 1845-57) featuring original furnishings, carpets, wallpaper, and Victorian-era pieces. The Drayton Plains one-room school house (c. 1865) contains an exhibit of its surroundings and of materials used in 1800s Michigan.

Port Huron

Port Huron Museum
Location: 1115 Sixth St, Port Huron, MI 48060.
Contact: (810) 982-0891, sbennett@phmuseum.org, www.phmuseum.org.
Hours: Daily 11am-5pm.
Admission: Adults $7, Seniors/Students $5, Family $20. Group tour rates for 20+ people, call (810) 982-0891

ext. 119 for reservations. *Site Info:* On-site parking. Wheelchair accessible. Free guide available. *Events:* Feast of St. Claire (Memorial Day weekend), World Festival (Sep), Friends of the Fort Gratiot Light Gala (May).

The Port Huron Museum began in 1972 in the Port Huron Public Library building built by Andrew Carnegie in 1904. With an emphasis on the maritime and local heritage of the Blue Water Area, the museum is the only multi-disciplinary organization in the area for arts, culture, and history. Exhibits include Great Lakes shipping artifacts, Russell Sawyer Photographs of local history, and the Robot Zoo: a biomechanical animal exhibit.

Thomas Edison Depot Museum
Location: Located under Blue Water Bridge.
Contact: (810) 455-0035. *Hours:* Memorial Day to Labor Day daily 11am-5pm, remainder of year Thurs-Mon 11am-5pm.
Admission: Adults $7, Seniors/Students $5, Family $20. Group tour rates for 20+ people, call (810) 982-0891 ext. 119 for reservations.
Site Info: On-site parking. Wheelchair accessible. Free guide available.

This depot is the Fort Gratiot station of the Grand Trunk Railroad where a teenage Thomas Edison worked during his years in Port Huron and conducted some of his early experiments. The site includes interactive displays and experiments, the restored baggage car recreates his mobile chemistry lab, and the Black Mariah movie theater shows films about Edison.

Huron Lightship
Location: North side of Pine Grove Park on St. Clair River.
Contact: (810) 984-9769, lightship@phmuseum.org.
Hours: Memorial Day to Labor Day daily 11am-5pm, closed Oct 31-April 15. *Admission:* Adults $7, Seniors/Students $5, Family $20. Group tour rates available for 20+ people, call (810) 982-0891 ext. 119 for reservations. *Site Info:* Parking in Pine Grove Park baseball lot. Not wheelchair accessible. Free guide available. *Events:* Fog Horn Sounding Memorial Day, Independence Day, and Labor Day.

The Huron Lightship was a "floating lighthouse" and spent its entire career on the Great Lakes with 36 years in Port Huron. Retired in 1970, the ship has been refinished as a museum and traces the history of its service and those who served.

U.S. Coast Guard Cutter Bramble
Location: Acheson Ventures Seaway Terminal, 2336 Military St.
Contact: (810) 434-8193, bramble@phmuseum.org.
Hours: Memorial Day to Labor Day Sat-Sun 11am-5pm.
Admission: Adults $7, Seniors/Students $5, Family $20. Group tour rates for 20+ people, call (810) 982-0891 ext. 119 for reservations.
Site Info: On-site parking. Not wheelchair accessible. Free guide available. *Events:* Bramble Overnights allow 20 or more to sleep on the ship while learning of its history; call reservation number for info. Ghost Ship Bramble (Oct).

Decommissioned in 2003, the USCG Cutter Bramble Museum Ship recreates life aboard the ship through sounds, ship models, and volunteer guides. This historic vessel was one of three to navigate the Northwest Passage through the Arctic Circle in 1957.

Presque Isle

Presque Isle Township Museum
Location: 4500 E. Grand Lake Rd., Presque Isle, MI 49777.
Contact: (989) 595-9917, chemiman@voyager.net, www.keepershouse.org. *Mail:* P.O. Box 208. *Events:* Independence and Labor Day Picnics.

The Presque Isle Township Museum Society supports and maintains two lighthouses and a lighthouse keeper's house (properties owned by Presque Isle Township).

New Presque Isle Lighthouse
Hours: May-Oct daily 9am-6pm. *Admission:* $2.50 to climb tower. 109-foot tower built in 1870. Active light maintained by U.S. Coast Guard

Keeper's Residence
Hours: Jun-Aug Tue-Sat 11am-5pm, Sun 1-5pm.
Built in 1905 when additional housing was required on site.
Maintained as a free museum by Presque Isle Museum Society.

Old Presque Isle Lighthouse
Hours: May-Oct daily 9am-6pm. *Admission:* $2.50.
Built in 1840. When the new lighthouse was built, this tower and the keeper's cottage were used as a summer cottage. The cottage shows the life of a lighthouse keeper and has maritime artifacts.

Prudenville

Houghton Lake Area Historical Village
Location: 1701 W. Houghton Lake Dr., Prudenville, MI 48651.
Contact: (989) 422-6393, crystalpines@i2k.com, www.houghtonlakehistory.com. *Mail:* P.O. Box 14, Houghton Lake, MI 48629. *Hours:* Summer Sat-Sun 12-4pm. *Admission:* Adults $3, Children 12 & under free. *Site Info:* On-site parking. Wheelchair accessible. Self-guided. *Events:* Historic Village Days (Aug).
The 13-building historic village replicates a 19th century logging-era community featuring a school museum, 1-mile nature trail, and operating general store. The adjacent historical playhouse was built in 1927 as Johnson Dance Hall. Collection includes photographs and memorabilia concerning logging in the area and Douglas Houghton's surveying tools.

Richmond

Bailey Park
Location: 36045 Park St., Richmond, MI 48062.
Contact: lln7210@gmail.com, www.richmondhistoricalsociety.org.
Mail: P.O. Box 68. *Hours:* By appointment. *Admission:* Adults $2, Children 5-12 $1, under 5 free.
Site Info: Street parking, small lot by cabin. Partially wheelchair accessible. Docents available by  request. *Events:* Log Cabin Day (Jun), Good Old Days (weekend after Labor Day).
This museum complex at Bailey Park, administered by the Richmond Area Historical Society, includes an 1885 one-room schoolhouse, 1915

Grand Trunk railroad depot, 1850 log cabin, and a replica of a blacksmith shop with a museum on the first floor. The schoolhouse has replica 1880s desks, dunce cap, and stool. The museum display changes annually in the fall.

Rochester Hills

Rochester Hills Museum at Van Hoosen Farm
Location: 1005 Van Hoosen Rd., Rochester Hills, MI 48306.
Contact: (248) 656-4663, rhmuseum@rochesterhills.org,
www.rochesterhills.org/museum.htm. *Hours:* Public hours: Fri-Sat 1-4pm. Business hours: Mon-Fri 8:30am-5pm. *Admission:* Adults $5, Seniors and students $3. *Site Info:* On-site parking. Wheelchair accessble.
Events: Vintage Baseball, Peter Rabbit Tea, Garden Tour, Homes Tour, Pumpkin Festival, Christmas activities, summer camps.
This 16-acre museum complex within Stoney Creek Village includes structures original to the property: the 1840 Van Hoosen farmhouse, 1850 red house, 1927 dairy barn, gardens, ponds, Stoney Creek, gazebo, barn, and buildings. Exhibits highlight settlement, agriculture, industry, and the cultural evolution of this community.

Rockford

Algoma Township Historical Displays
Location: 10531 Algoma Ave, Rockford, MI 49341.
Contact: (616) 866-1583, algomaplan@chartermi.net,
www.algomatwp.org/historical_society.htm. *Hours:* Mon-Fri 8:30am-4:30pm.
The Algoma Township Historical Society gathers and catalogs historical artifacts and archival materials for display in four cases at the township offices.

Rockford Area Historical Museum
Location: 11 E. Bridge St., Rockford, MI 49341.
Contact: (616) 886-2235, vic@pathwaynet.com,
www.rockfordmuseum.org. *Mail:* P.O. Box 781. *Hours:* Jun-Sep Thurs-Sat 1-4pm, also by appointment. *Admission:* Free. *Events:* Scarecrow making (Oct).
The museum occupies the 1903 Rouge River Electric Light and Power building next to the dam.

Rogers City

Forty Mile Point Lighthouse

Location: Presque Isle County
Lighthouse Park, 7323 US-23 N,
Rogers City, MI 48779.
Contact: (989) 734-4587,
barbara71@Hughes.net,
www.40milepointlighthouse.org.
Mail: P.O. Box 205.
Hours: Memorial Day-Oct Tue-
Sun 10am-4pm. *Admission:* Free.
Events: Memorial Day Weekend
Open House and Night at the Lighthouse (Oct).
An 1896 brick "mirror image" keepers' quarters, providing housing for
two families, is centered by an attached 59-foot-high light tower with a
4th order Fresnel lens. Also onsite are the pilot house of the steamer
Calcite, restored to serve as a nautical show-piece and link to area's
nautical past, and the wreck of the Joseph S. Fay.

Presque Isle County Historical Museum

Location: 176 W. Michigan, Rogers City, MI 49779.
Contact: (989) 734-4121, bradleymuseum@yahoo.com,
www.thebradleyhouse.org. *Mail:* P.O. Box 175. *Hours:* May-Sep Tue-Sat
12-4pm Also by appointment. *Admission:* Free. *Site Info:* Street parking.
Not handicap accessible. Live guide available. *Events:* Nautical Festival
(Aug), Christmas at Bradley House (Thanksgiving to New Year).
The Society was organized in 1954 to preserve artifacts from Great Lakes
shipping, Indian culture, and limestone production and acquired the 1914
Bradley House in 1980. Carl D. Bradley was first of a series of executives
of Michigan Limestone and Chemical Company to use the house. Three
floors of exhibits include the Bradley dining room, Victorian music room,
Bertram Sister's Millinery Shop, country store, schoolroom, and a Bradley
Transportation Line display with a model of the ill-fated Carl D. Bradley.
The collection includes 40,000 photos from the calcite plant beginning in
1911, the Steward Collection of 24,000 images, and various books and
files of local history. Call in advance to use collections.

Romeo

Romeo Arts and Archives Center

Location: 290 N. Main St., Romeo, MI 48065.
Contact: (586) 752-4111, www.libcoop.net/romrhs. *Mail:* P.O. Box 412.
Hours: Tue 7-9pm. *Admission:* Free. *Site Info:* Free on-site parking.
Wheelchair accessible. Guided tours by appointment. *Events:* Victorian
Festival (May), Cemetery Walk (Oct), Holiday Home Tour (Dec).
The Romeo Historical Society maintains this museum dedicated to
preserving Romeo history as well as the Clyde Craig Blacksmith Museum
(301 N. Bailey Street) and the 1868 Bancroft-Stranahan Home (132
Church Street) with period furnishings.

Roscommon

Civilian Conservation Corps Museum
Location: 11747 N. Higgins Lake Dr., Roscommon, MI 48653.
Contact: (989) 275-5835, www.michigan.gov/cccmuseum. *Hours:* May-Sep daily 10am-4pm. *Admission:* State Park Motor Vehicle Permit.
Site Info: Call (989) 348-2537 to schedule a tour. *Events:* See website.
More than 100,000 young men worked in Michigan's forests during the Great Depression and lived in barracks like this. See how "Roosevelt's tree army" served the state, creating a legacy that we enjoy today.

Gallimore Boarding House
Location: 416 Lake St., Roscommon, MI 48653.
Contact: (989) 275-5835. *Mail:* P.O. Box 916. *Hours:* Memorial Day-Sep Fri-Sat 12-4pm. *Admission:* Free. *Site Info:* Free street parking.
Wheelchair accessible. Docent available.
The Roscommon Area Historical Society maintains this museum in the historic boarding house, which operated from 1904-1931, as a museum containing four rooms furnished to that period. A one-story addition on the back replicates the original kitchen and a dining room. Another museum is located in the Richardson Schoolhouse, 1914-1955.

Royal Oak

Royal Oak Historical Society Museum
Location: 1415 West Webster Rd., Royal Oak, MI 48073.
Contact: (248) 439-1501, curator@royaloakhistoricalsociety.org, www.royaloakhistoricalsociety.com. *Hours:* Tue, Thurs, & Sat 1-4pm, 2nd and 4th Sun 1-4pm. *Admission:* $2 donation. *Site Info:* On-site parking. Wheelchair accessible. Group tours by appointment.
Events: Memorial Day Pancake Breakfast at Farmers' Market, Annual Dinner.
The museum relocated to the 1927 Fire Station building in 2010. Exhibits change every 3-4 months. Artifacts include historical objects, documents, pictures, and books from 1830 onward.

St. Clair

St. Clair Historical Museum
Location: 304 S. Fourth St., Clair, MI 48079.
Contact: (810) 329-6888, traveler135@aol.com. *Hours:* Year-round Tue 9:30am-12pm, also Sat-Sun 1:30-4:30pm in May-Oct.
Admission: Donations accepted. *Site Info:* Free on-site parking. Not wheelchair accessible. Free tours by appointment, call (810)-329-4574.
Events: Monthly summer programs.
An appointed commission is dedicated to preserving St. Clair history and maintains this museum featuring a marine display, Diamond Crystal Salt room, Brenner Shoe Shop, Native American display, and many items pertaining to the city.

St. Clair Shores

Selinsky-Green Farmhouse Museum
Location: 22500 Eleven Mile Rd., St. Clair Shores, MI 48081.
Contact: (586) 771-9020, stachowm@libcoop.net. *Hours:* Sep-May Wed & Sat 1-4pm, Jun-Aug Wed 1-4pm. *Admission:* Donations accepted.
Site Info: Nearby parking. Guides available upon request.
Events: Tea Party.
Prussian immigrants, John and Mary Selinsky, came to St. Clair Shores (then Erin Township) in 1868 and by 1874 had built this log, salt-box farmhouse. The museum features changing exhibits, period-decorated rooms, guided tours, and special events.

St. Johns

Paine-Gilliam-Scott Museum
Location: 106 Maple St., St. Johns, MI 48879.
Contact: (989) 224-2894, pgsmuseum@hotmail.com, www.pgsmuseum.com. *Mail:* 100 E. State St. *Hours:* Mid-Apr to Dec Sun 1-4pm & Wed 2-7pm. *Admission:* Donations accepted.
Site Info: Street parking. Not wheelchair accessible. Guides available.
This 1860 furnished house museum, maintained by the Clinton County Historical Society, examines Clinton County history and Joseph Campau history related to the county. The museum carriage house has agricultural and industrial displays. Also features a doctor's office, driver's quarters, and Swegles General Store.

St. Joseph

Heritage Museum and Cultural Center
Location: 601 Main St., St. Joseph, MI 49085.
Contact: (269) 983-1191, kenpott@theheritagemcc.org, www.theheritagemcc.org. *Hours:* Tue-Fri 10am-4pm, also Sun 12-4pm Jun-Sep. Library by appointment. *Admission:* Adults $5, Members/Youth free. *Site Info:* Free parking. Wheelchair accessible. *Events:* Monthly programs (see website).
The center encompasses an exhibit area and a research library with archives containing books, reference volumes, periodicals, maps, manuscripts, business records, photo and postcard collections, slides, oral history tapes, vintage film and genealogical records focused on the St. Joseph-Benton Harbor region and its place in Michigan and Great Lakes history.

St. Louis

St. Louis Historic Park
Location: 110 E. Crawford St., St. Louis, MI 48880.
Contact: (989) 681-3071, stlouisdda@stlouismi.com,
www.stlouismi.com/1/stlouis/Historical_Society.asp. *Mail:* Philip
Hansen, City of St. Louis, 108 W. Saginaw St. *Hours:* Thurs 1-4pm, also
by appointment. *Admission:* Donations accepted. *Site Info:* On-site
parking. Wheelchair accessible. Guides available. *Events:* Strawberry
Shortcake Sale.
The 1873 Pere Marquette railroad depot was restored in 2008 by the St.
Louis Area Historical Society as part of a historic park including a
transportation pavilion and plank road toll booth. A log cabin sits across
from the depot at 119 E. Crawford. Exhibits feature local historical
artifacts including a restored 1917 Republic Truck built in Alma, a hand-
carved canoe from the 1880s and a restored fire department hose reel.

Saginaw

Castle Museum of
Saginaw County
History
Location: 500 Federal Ave.,
Saginaw, MI 48607.
Contact: (989) 752-2861,
ksanta@castlemuseum.org,
www.castlemuseum.org.
Hours: Tue-Sat 10am-
4:30pm, Sun 1-4:30pm.
Admission: $1 Adults, $0.50

Youth, HSSC Members free. *Site Info:* Free on-site and street parking.
Wheelchair accessible. Guided tours by reservation. *Events:* Jazz on
Jefferson (Jun), Riverside Saginaw Film Festival, Holidays at the Castle.
The Historical Society of Saginaw County preserves the Castle Building
as well as telling the story of the people of the Saginaw area and their
cultural and historical heritage. The Castle Building, a former post office,
is a 3-story French chateau-like structure built in 1898. The society also
maintains Castle 201 across the street in former Jacobson's Department
Store. Traveling and permanent exhibits include a lumbering display, an
archaeology exhibit, and a model railroad exhibit with more than 1,000 ft.
of track.

Saginaw Railway Museum
Location: 900 Maple St., Saginaw, MI 48602.
Contact: (989) 790-7994, info@saginawrailwaymuseum.org,
www.saginawrailwaymuseum.org. *Mail:* P.O. Box 20454. *Hours:* Call for
dates and times. *Admission:* Donations accepted. *Site Info:* Free parking.
Partially wheelchair accessible. Guides available.
Dedicated to the preservation and enhancement of railroad lore and
technology, this museum is located in a 1907 Pere Marquette railway

depot moved to Saginaw in 1983. Featuring a Mershon interlocking tower, two cabooses, a retired RS-1 Alco locomotive, HO scale model layout in basement, passenger coach, C&O combine car, and a former US Navy 25-ton switch engine.

Salem

Jarvis Stone School
Location: 7991 N. Territorial Rd., Salem, MI 48175.
Contact: (248) 486-0669, salem_area_hs@yahoo.com, www.sahshistory.org. *Mail:* P.O. Box 75011. *Hours:* 4th Wed Apr, May, & Oct 7-9pm, also by appointment. *Admission:* Free. *Site Info:* Parking in grass lot next to school. Wheelchair accessible. Free guide available.
Events: Dinner/Auction (Feb), Barn Dance (Sep), Country Fair (Sep).
The Salem Area Historical Society took possession of the 1857 Jarvis Stone School in 1978 and is restoring the 1830s Dickerson Barn, the oldest barn in Washtenaw County.

Saline

Saline Depot Museum

Location: 402 N. Ann Arbor St., Saline, MI 48176.
Contact: (734) 944-0442, salinehistory@verizon.net, www.salinehistory.org.
Mail: P.O. Box 302.
Hours: Year-round Sat 11am-3pm. *Admission:* Free.
Site Info: Free parking. Call for wheelchair accessibility. Guide available, reservations required for 10+ people with $1/person fee. *Events:* Harvest Time (Oct), Christmas on the Farm (Dec).
Exhibits in the 1870 Victorian depot include pictures of historic depots, displays of Saline's history and town founder, the depot's original Fairbanks Scale, and a walking tour by the tracks. An 1830s livery barn and the Fairbanks Morse windmill behind it have been restored as well as a 1906 caboose furnished with small beds, a toilet, and a potbelly stove as used by trainmen. Maintained by the Saline Area Historical Society.

Rentschler Farm Museum
Location: 1265 E. Michigan Ave.
Hours: May to Dec Sat 11am-3pm. *Admission:* Free.
Site Info: Partially wheelchair accessible: first floor only. Guided house tour, reservations required for groups of 10 or more with a $1 per-person fee.
Established 1901 by Emanuel Rentschler, this farm was operated by 4 generations of the family until it was sold to the city in 1998. Leased to historical society, the site now includes a 12-room farmhouse furnished c. 1930, 10 outbuildings with tools, and live animals.

Bixby Marionette Exhibit

Location: Saline District Library, 555 N. Maple, Saline, MI 48176.
Contact: 734/429-5450, grossmanfamily1@verizon.net,
www.salinechamber.com/bixby_puppets.htm. *Hours:* Mon-Thurs 9am-9
pm, Fri-Sat 10am-5pm, Sun 1pm-5pm. *Admission:* Free. *Site Info:* Free
parking. Wheelchair accessible. Guided tour by appointment.
Events: Puppetry Arts Festival held in conjunction with Harvest of the
Arts/Octoberfest.
An exhibit at Saline District Library celebrates Meredith Bixby, a Saline
native son and one of America's foremost puppeteers. Permanent display
on the making of a marionette, is complemented by a changing display of
scenes (3 exhibits per year, Jan-May-Sep).

Sanford

Sanford Centennial Museum

Location: 2222 Smith St., Sanford, MI 48657.
Contact: (989) 687-9048, (989) 687-5327, www.sanfordhist.org.
Mail: P.O. Box 243. *Hours:* Memorial Day to Labor Day Sat 10am-5pm,
Sun 1-5pm, also by appointment. *Admission:* Free. *Site Info:* On-site
parking. Partially wheelchair accessible. Self-guided, guided tours by
appointment. *Events:* Log Cabin Day (Jun), Founders Day (Sep).
The museum includes restored and furnished historic buildings: two
schools, a general store, log cabin, township hall, church, train depot and
train. Inside the buildings are vintage tools, implements from the logging
days, political memorabilia, a dentist's office, a saloon, toys, and
household goods.

Saugatuck

Saugatuck-Douglas Historical Museum

Location: 735 Park St.,
Saugatuck, MI 49453.
Contact: (269) 857-7901,
(269) 897-7900,
info@sdhistoricalsociety.org,
www.sdhistoricalsociety.org.
Mail: P.O. Box 617, Douglas,
MI 49406. *Hours:* Memorial
Day to Labor Day: Daily 12-4 pm. Labor Day-Oct: Sat-Sun 12-4 pm.
Admission: Donations accepted. *Site Info:* Free parking. Wheelchair
accessible. Self-guided walking tours (maps available). *Events:* Heritage
Festival (Sep).
The Saugatuck-Douglas Historical Society preserves, collects and
presents area history, arts, and geography and is developing a Discovery
Center in the 1866 Douglas Union School. Exhibits focus on local history
and industry.

Sebewaing

Sebewaing Area Historical Society
Location: 15 Sharpsteen St., Sebewaing, MI 48759.
Contact: (989) 883-2391, (989) 883-2341, djbeers@sebewaing.net,
sebewaingchamber.com. *Hours:* May-Oct weekends 1-3pm, also by
appointment. *Admission:* Donations accepted. *Events:* Michigan Sugar
Festival, Ice Cream Social, Christmas Open House, Midnight Madness.
Operates two facilities.

> ### Old Sebewaing Township Hall
> *Location:* 92 S. Center St.
> This former 1877 Township Hall includes the office, jail, jury room,
> voting booths, and many displays of local industry including fishing,
> the sugar factory, and local doctors.

> ### Charles W. Liken Museum
> *Location:* 325 N. Center St.
> One of five homes built by Liken, this residence was enlarged for use
> as a funeral home. The site includes a Victorian dining room,
> merchant displays, clothing displays, and a working kitchen.

Shepherd

Shepherd Area Historical Society Museum
Location: 314 W. Maple St., Shepherd, MI 48883.
Contact: (989) 828-5319. *Mail:* P.O. Box 505. *Hours:* Open during
meetings and Maple Syrup festival, also by appointment. *Admission:* Free.
Site Info: Street parking. Self-guided. *Events:* Maple Syrup Festival (Apr),
Ice Cream Social and Central Michigan Area Band concert (Jul).
The society maintains this museum and "The Little Red Schoolhouse,"
located on the high school grounds on East Hall Street.

Sidney

North Sidney Church and Cemetery

Location: 1990 S. Grow Rd.,
Sidney, MI 48885.
Contact: www.northsidney.com.
Mail: P.O. Box 202.
Hours: Open for Memorial Day
Service and special occasions.
Admission: Donations accepted.
Site Info: Street parking. Not wheelchair accessible. Guide available upon
request. *Events:* Memorial Day Service.
Built as St. John's Church in 1903 after tornado destroyed the original
Danish emigrant church building, its collection includes bibles, photos of
the church and families, and a "Heritage Wall."

South Haven

Historical Association of South Haven
Location: 355 Hubbard St., South Haven, MI 49090.
Contact: (269) 637-6424, info@historyofsouthhaven.org,
www.historyofsouthhaven.org. *Mail:* P.O. Box 552. *Hours:* Hartman
School tours Memorial Day-Oct Sun 2-4pm. *Admission:* Free.
Site Info: Street parking. Self-guided. *Events:* "Celebrating Michigan's
History" Day, Sherman's Ice Cream Social (Jun).
Formed in 2002 to promote understanding of South Haven history, the
association maintains exhibits and archives in Hartman School.

Liberty Hyde Bailey Museum
Location: 903 S. Bailey Ave, South Haven, MI 49090.
Contact: (269) 637-3251, lhbm@south-haven.com, www.lhbm.south-
haven.com. *Hours:* Mar-Dec Thurs-Mon 1-5pm, Jan-Feb Sat-Sun 1-5pm,
also by appointment. Gardens and nature walk open from dawn to dusk.
Admission: Free. *Site Info:* Free parking in hospital lot. Wheelchair
accessible. Guides available, group and school tours by appointment.
Events: Mothers' Day Kousa Dogwood Sale, South Haven Garden Club
Walk (Jul), Brown Bag biology sessions (Summer), Blueberry Festival
(Aug).
This birthplace of "America's Father of Modern Horticulture," Dr. Liberty
Hyde Bailey, demonstrates the links between botany, horticulture,
agriculture, and everyday life. Includes artifacts and documents pertaining
both to Bailey and his family and to South Haven history.

Michigan Flywheelers Museum
Location: 06285 68th St., South
Haven, MI 49090-7147.
Contact: (269) 639-2010,
michiganflywheelers@yahoo.com,
www.michiganflywheelers.org.
Mail: 64958 Hwy. M-43, Bangor,
MI 49013. *Hours:* Memorial Day
Weekend to Labor Day Wed & Sat-
Sun 10am-3pm, also by appointment.
Admission: By donation.
Site Info: Free on-site parking.
Wheelchair accessible. Free guide
available. *Events:* Swap Meet and
Flea Market (Jun), South Haven
Bluegrass Festival (Aug), Antique Engine and Tractor Show (Sep),
Christmas at the Flywheelers (Nov).
Dedicated to the preservation of antique farm equipment, this 80-acre
museum contains an Old Towne area with businesses like "Over The Hill"
Forge, Old Town Jail, and Abbert and Son Machinery Repair. Exhibits
include a log cabin, shingle mill, saw mill, wooden nickel gift shop, and
migrant worker camp.

South Lyon

Green Oak Township Heritage Museum
Location: Historic 1856 Township Hall, 10789 Silver Lake Rd., South Lyon, MI 48178.
Contact: (248) 437-8416, (248) 939-2901, jowilliams@aol.com, gail.huck@charter.net, www.greenoaktownshiphistorical society.com. *Hours:* By appointment. *Events:* Green Oak Day (Aug).
The museum, located in an addition to the 1856 Green Oak Township Hall, includes the hall's original meeting room which is undergoing restoration for public activities. The museum's collection includes histories of 8 one-room schools in the township, a growing library, and many artifacts from the 1800s.

Witch's Hat Historic Village and Museum
Location: Mc Hattie Park, 300 Dorothy St., South Lyon, MI 48178.
Contact: (248) 437-9929, dfwynings@sbcglobal.net, www.southlyonmi.org/1/223/ history_of_south_lyon.asp.
Mail: P.O. Box 263.
Hours: Apr-Nov Thurs-Sun 1-

4pm. *Admission:* Free. *Site Info:* Free parking. Guides available by appointment. *Events:* Depot Day (Sep).
Operated by South Lyon Area Historical Society volunteers and accredited by the American Association of Museums, the Historic Village includes a 1909 Queen Anne's depot, freight house, a wooden caboose, the 1907 Washburn School, a 1930s chapel, and a gazebo.

Sterling Heights

Upton House
Location: Sterling Heights Library, 40255 Dodge Park Rd, Sterling Heights, MI 48313.
Contact: (586) 446-2640, turgeant@libcoop.net, www.shpl.net/histcom.html. *Hours:* Open during Sterlingfest (Aug) and Sterling Christmas (Dec). *Admission:* Free. *Site Info:* Parking in city lot. Partially wheelchair accessible: first floor only. Self-guided.
The Sterling Heights Historical Commission and the library install exhibits in this Italianate 1867 home. The collection includes maps, photographs, and documents relating to personal, business, educational, cultural, and recreational activities.

Sturgis

Sturgis Historical Society
Location: 200 W. Main St., Sturgis, MI 49091.
Contact: (616) 651-8854, relics@charter.net. *Mail:* P.O. Box 392.
Hours: Mon-Fri 8:30am-4:40pm. *Admission:* Free. *Events:* Ice Cream
Social (Aug).
The museum shares the former railroad depot with the local Chamber of
Commerce. Its collection contains 1,500 Sturgis area items including a
motorhome built from a Spartan bus.

Taylor

Taylor Heritage Park
Location: Pardee Rd. between
Goddard and Northland,
Taylor, MI 48180.
Contact: (734) 287-3835,
ggouth@comcast.net.
Mail: P.O. Box 1225.
Hours: Tue-Sun 12-6 pm.
Admission: Free. *Site Info:* Free
parking. Wheelchair accessible.

Guides available, contact for info. *Events:* Taylor Days, July fireworks,
Log Cabin Day, Art Fair, Octoberfest.
The Taylor Historical Society preserves, restores, collects, and displays
historical sites and personal property relating to the City of Taylor, its
people, government, and organization. Attractions include the train station
in Heritage Park, a 1920s House, and a one-room schoolhouse. The 1882
schoolhouse is fully equipped with historic teaching tools and McGuffey
Readers.

Tecumseh

Tecumseh Area Historical Museum
Location: 302 E. Chicago Blvd., Tecumseh, MI 49286.
Contact: (517) 423-2374, historictecumseh@gmail.com,
www.historictecumseh.com. *Mail:* P.O. Box 26. *Hours:* Wed-Sat 11am-
3pm. *Admission:* Free. *Site Info:* On-site parking. Guides available.
Events: Vets Concert, Basket Sale (May).
The museum is housed in the historic St. Elizabeth's Catholic Church: a
small, Gothic-style building constructed in 1913. This beautifully restored
fieldstone building contains a wealth of area history and artifacts
including a Dynamic Kernel exhibit, Meyers-Divers Airport exhibit, and
artifacts from the Underground Railroad. It also contains significant
materials concerning the history and cultural impact of the automobile,
industrial manufacturing and design, and other aspects of American
culture.

Temperance

Banner Oak School
Location: Sterns Rd. and Crabb Rd., Temperance, MI 48182.
Contact: (734) 847-6171, lindaski@buckeye-access.com. *Mail:* 1430
Granby St. *Hours:* Apr-Oct by appointment. *Admission:* Free.
Site Info: On-site parking. *Events:* Colonial Craft Show (Dec).
The Bedford Historical Society restored and refurnished this 1871 one-room school.

Traverse City

Grand Traverse Heritage Center

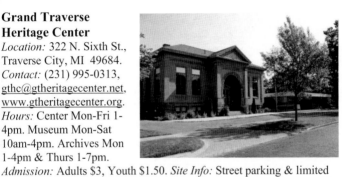

Location: 322 N. Sixth St.,
Traverse City, MI 49684.
Contact: (231) 995-0313,
gthc@gtheritagecenter.net,
www.gtheritagecenter.org.
Hours: Center Mon-Fri 1-
4pm. Museum Mon-Sat
10am-4pm. Archives Mon
1-4pm & Thurs 1-7pm.
Admission: Adults $3, Youth $1.50. *Site Info:* Street parking & limited
on-site parking. Wheelchair accessible. Self-guided. *Events:* Haig Golf
Outing, Festival of Model Trains, Education Heritage Days.
The Heritage Center, located in a former Carnegie Library, maintains a
museum on Grand Traverse history. Also in the center are offices of
historical and heritage organizations, including the Traverse Area
Historical Society, the Railroad Historical Society of Northwest
Michigan, the Grand Traverse Rock and Mineral Club, and the Women's
History Project of Northwest Michigan. Archives maintained by the
Traverse Area Historical Society include more than 13,000 photos,
documents, and newspaper clippings related to regional history. The
building also houses the former Con Foster Museum collection which
numbers over 10,000 artifacts donated by the residents of Grand Traverse
region since 1935.

Trenton

Trenton Historical Museum
Location: 306 St. Joseph St., Trenton, MI 48183.
Contact (734) 675-2130, www.trentonhistoricalcommission.org.
Mail: 2800 Third St. *Hours:* Feb-Jul & Sep-Dec Sat 1-4pm.
Admission: Donations accepted. *Site Info:* Parking on 3rd St. and St.
Joseph. Not wheelchair accessible. Self-guided. *Events:* Trenton Mid-
Summer Festival (Jul), Victorian Christmas (Dec).

The museum is located in a Victorian style home built in 1881 by John and Sarah Moore. Decorated in the style of the Victorian period, it also contains information on the history of Trenton and area artifacts.

Vassar

Watrousville Museum
Location: 4607 W. Caro Rd. (M-81), Vassar, MI 48768.
Contact: (989) 823-2360, dave@watrousville.com,
www.watrousville.com. *Mail:* P.O. Box 15, Caro, MI 48723. *Hours:* Jun-Sep Thurs 1-4 pm, also by appointment. *Admission:* Donations accepted.
Site Info: Free parking. Guides available. *Events:* Founder's Day Banquet (Sep).
The museum, located in the Watrous General Store building, preserves history from the 1850s forward. The Watrousville-Caro Area Historical Society is currently restoring the 1858 McGlone House for a museum addition. The 80-foot "Lincoln Pole" from Abraham Lincoln's second presidential campaign may be the last in the U.S.

Vicksburg

Vicksburg Depot Museum
Location: 300 N. Richardson St., Vicksburg, MI 49097.
Contact: (269) 649-1733, vixmus1@yahoo.com,
www.vicksburghistory.org. *Mail:* P.O. Box 103. *Hours:* May-Dec Sat 10am-3pm. *Admission:* Free. *Site Info:* On-site parking. Partially wheelchair accessible. Free guided tours by appointment. *Events:* Harvest Festival (Sep).
Administered by the Vicksburg Historical Society, this museum is housed in a restored 1905 Vicksburg Grand Trunk depot. Additionally, the Historic Village includes the restored one-room Strong School, a 1940s print shop/newspaper office, the 1910 Oswal farmstead, a caboose and boxcar, and a township hall building that dates to the early 1900s. Exhibits showcase Village of Vicksburg history as well as train history.

Warren

Bunert School
Location: 27900 Bunert Rd.,
Warren, MI 48092.
Contact: warrenhistsoc@yahoo.com.
Hours: 1st Sun of month 1-4pm
(closed Jan-Feb Jul & Sep) also by
appointment. *Admission:* Free.
Site Info: Parking near entrance.
Wheelchair accessible. Self-guided.

This restored one-room school is maintained by the Warren Historical and Genealogical Society and features exhibits detailing the years 1875-1944.

Warren Historical Gallery

Location: Warren Community Center, 5460 Arden Rd., Warren, MI 48092.
Contact: (586) 258-2056, histcommm@cityofwarren.org. *Hours:* Gallery Mon-Fri 9am-5pm, also by appointment. Hallway displays 9am-9pm.
Admission: Free. *Site Info:* Parking near entrance. Wheelchair accessible. Self-guided, contact for group tour info.
These displays, maintained through the cooperation of the Warren Historical Commission and the Warren Historical and Genealogical Society, describe local history from the time of "The Impassable Swamp" circa 1817 to Warren today. Hallway displays are rotated quarterly.

Washington

Washington Historical Museum

Location: 58230 VanDyke, Washington, MI 48094.
Contact: (586) 786-5304, (248) 652-2458, washhistsoc@yahoo.com, www.washhistsoc.org. *Mail:* P.O. Box 94144. *Hours:* Jun-Nov 2nd & 4th Sun 1-4pm. *Site Info:* Guided tours, call (586) 677-1587.
Events: Washington's birthday (Feb), Art and Craft Show (Jun).
The Greater Washington Area Historical Society maintains a museum in the former 1916 Washington High School. Exhibits in five rooms focus on the Freedom Shrine, the Washington area, military displays, George Washington, sports, and period rooms. A Scouting Museum covers 75 years including uniforms and memoribillia.

Loren Andrus Octagon House

Location: 57500 VanDyke Ave., Washington, MI 48094.
Contact: (586) 781-0084, info@octagonhouse.org, www.octagonhouse.org. *Mail:* P.O. Box 94118. *Hours:* Feb-Oct 2nd & 4th Sun 12-4pm, groups by appointment. *Admission:* $5 per person.
Site Info: Free parking. Self-guided. *Events:* Open Houses (Nov-Dec).
This 1860s home was inspired by Orson Squire Fowler's publication "The Octagon House: A Home for All." The house is on an old Underground Railroad route and had been used for a variety of different endeavors, ranging from an inn to the Wayne State University agricultural program. The house and grounds have been restored to the Victorian era.

Waterford

Historic Waterford Village

Location: 4490 Hatchery Rd., Waterford, MI 48330.
Contact: (248) 683-2697, sstrait649@comcast.net, www.waterfordhistoricalsociety.org.
Mail: P.O. Box 300491. *Hours:* Wed 10:30am-2pm. *Admission:* Free.
Site Info: On-site parking. Wheelchair accessible. Guided tours.
Events: Log Cabin Days (Jun), Christmas in October.

This 1900s village includes a 1919 home, log cabin, Drayton's Plain depot, Grand Trunk caboose, carriage house, millinery shop, barber shop, print shop, woodworking shop, doctor and dentist office, bakery, the 1919 Hatchery House, and a replica of the J.R. Jones General Store in Greenfield Village that store once stood in Waterford and was named Jacober's General Store.

Wayne

City of Wayne Historical Museum
Location: NE Biddle and Main St., Wayne, MI 48184.
Contact: (734) 722-0113, museum@ci.wayne.mi.us,
www.ci.wayne.mi.us/historical_museum.shtml. *Mail:* 1 Town Sq.
Hours: Fri-Sat 1-4pm, Mon-Thurs by appointment.
Admission: Free. *Site Info:* Lot or Street parking. Wheelchair accessible. Self-guided.
Opened in 1964 in the former city offices, the museum contains over 100 exhibits tracing the path from village to city.

West Branch

Ogemaw Genealogical and Historical Society Museum
Location: 123 S. 5th St., West Branch, MI 48661.
Contact: (989) 873-5673, zettle@sbcglobal.net, oghs-info
@ejourney.com, www.westbranch.com/ogemaw_genealogical.htm.
Mail: P.O. Box 734. *Hours:* Thurs-Fri 10am-2pm, also by appointment.
Admission: Free. *Site Info:* On-site parking. Not wheelchair accessible.
Call for group tour info. *Events:* Nancy Douglas Doll and Tea Party (Jul), driving tours.
Reflective of 19th and 20th century Ogemaw County, this museum highlights toys, household goods, decorative arts, rural schools, business, the oil industry, Native Americans, lumbering, military, music, and an extensive photographic collection. "The Music of Ogemaw County" features local music history from Native Americans to community, church, and school music. "WWII: Overseas and at Home" tells the story of Ogemaw County's role in WWII.

White Lake

Kelley-Fisk Farm
Location: 9180 Highland Rd., White Lake, MI 48383.
Contact: (248) 360-0188, gregrbaroni@aol.com,
www.whitelakehistory.org. *Mail:* 7525 Highland Rd. *Hours:* By appointment or for special events. *Events:* Farmers Market (daily May-Oct), Fisk Farm Days (Sep), Christmas on the Farm (Dec).
The White Lake Historical Society's 1855 Kelley-Fisk Farm includes a

Greek Revival farmhouse and outbuildings (a barn, pig and hen houses, two corn cribs, garage, and a privy). The 1876 Thompson one-room school was also moved to the site in 1995.

White Pigeon

U.S. Land Office
Location: 113 W. Chicago Rd., White Pigeon, MI 49099.
Contact: (269) 503-0196, mstarmann@yahoo.com.
Mail: P.O. Box 492, Centreville, MI 49032.
Hours: By appointment.
Admission: Free. *Site Info:* On-site parking. Not wheelchair accessible. Self-guided.

This restored 1830 building houses the St. Joseph County Historical Society's collection including items pertaining to native and local history and items from the collection of the Pioneer Society.

Wyandotte

Wyandotte Historical Museum
Location: 2624 Biddle Ave, Wyandotte, MI 48192.
Contact: (734) 324-7284, museum@wyan.org, www.wyandottemuseums.org. *Hours:* Tours Apr-Dec Thurs-Sun 12-4pm.
Admission: Adults $2, Youth $0.50. *Site Info:* Free parking. Wheelchair accessible. Guided tours. *Events:* Heritage Events Series: Monthly events throughout the year that celebrate the heritage and culture of the City of Wyandotte (see website).
The main exhibit building, housed in the 1896 Ford-MacNichol Home, features a wrap-around porch, tower, six fireplaces, original oak woodwork, and period décor. Seasonal exhibits and period vignettes highlight the Museum's collection of 19th century furnishings, clothing, and local history artifacts. The museum's campus of three historic buildings also offers local history archives.

Ypsilanti

Yankee Air Museum
Location: Willow Run Airport, W. Hanger II., Ypsilanti.
Contact: (734) 483-4030, gayle.drews@yankeeairmuseum.org, www.yankeeairmuseum.org. *Mail:* P.O. Box 590, Belleville, MI 48112.
Hours: Tue-Fri 10am-4pm. *Events:* Our Hearts Go Out To Yankee Dinner and Auction (Feb), Italian Bistro Dinner and Dance (Apr), Memorial Day Observance, Thunder Over Michigan Air Show (Aug).

Hangar tours include historic flyable aircraft and military vehicles under restoration. FLEX rides may be taken in restored military aircraft (contact museum for availability and restrictions). The museum coordinates activities with re-enactors and the military vehicle owner community to provide living history equipment and personnel for events and air shows. Education and oral history programs provide an opportunity to experience, preserve, and embark upon aviation and military history. Nearby, the restored 1938 Willow Run School, built by Henry Ford, houses education programs.

Zeeland

Zeeland Historical Museum
Location: 37 E. Main St., Zeeland, MI 49464.
Contact: (616) 772-4079, dekker@sirus.com, www.zeelandmuseum.org.
Mail: P.O. Box 165. *Hours:* Mar-Oct Thurs 10am-7pm, Sat 10am-2pm, business hours by appointment. *Admission:* Free. *Site Info:* Free parking. Self-guided, tours available by appointment. *Events:* Historic Home Tour. The museum complex includes a restored 1876 house and store formerly owned by Dirk Dekker; a barn with farm implements and a Zeeland hatcheries display; and an interurban station. The New Groningen School is undergoing restoration. Exhibits include a log cabin, Dutch immigration, a market, the first Zeeland Bank, and a Victorian parlor.

Cross Index

Capac Community Museum and Kempf Historical Center	LP	Capac
Capitol Hill School	LP	Marshall
Cappon House Museum	LP	Holland
Cascade Museum	LP	Alto
Cascade History Room	LP	Grand Rapids
Caseville Historical Museum	LP	Caseville
Castle Museum of Saginaw County History	LP	Saginaw
Centrall Mine Village	UP	Eagle Harbor
Centreville Museum and Historic Library	LP	Centreville
Charles H. Wright Museum of African American History	LP	Detroit
Charles W. Liken Museum	LP	Sebewaing
Chassell Heritage Center	UP	Chassell
Cheboygan County Historical Museum	LP	Cheboygan
Chesaning Historical Museum	LP	Chesaning
Chesterfield Museum and Historic Village	LP	Chesterfield
Chippewa County Museum	UP	Sault Ste Marie
City of Wayne Historical Museum	LP	Wayne
Civilian Conservation Corps Museum	LP	Roscommon
Clarke Historical Library	LP	Mt Pleasant
Clarkston Heritage Museum	LP	Clarkston
Clinton Township Historical Village	LP	Clinton Twp.
Cobach Center	LP	Brighton
Colonial Michilimackinac	LP	Mackinaw City
Coopersville Area Historical Society Museum	LP	Coopersville
Copper Harbor Lighthouse	UP	Copper Harbor
Copper Range Historical Museum	UP	South Range
Coppertown USA Mining Museum	UP	Calumet
Covington Township Historical Museum	UP	Covington
Crawford County Museum	LP	Grayling
Crocker House Museum	LP	Mount Clemens
Curtis Historical Society Museum	UP	Curtis
Custom House Museum	LP	Grosse Ile
Davis Brothers Farm Shop Museum	LP	Lapeer
Dearborn Historical Museum	LP	Dearborn
Delta County Historical Museum	UP	Escanaba
Depot Transportation Museum	LP	Grand Haven
DeTour Passage Historical Museum	UP	DeTour Village
Detroit Historical Museum	LP	Detroit
Dewey School	LP	Grass Lake
Dexter Area Historical Society and Museum	LP	Dexter
D&M Railroad Depot	LP	Millersburg
Dossin Great Lakes Museum	LP	Detroit
Dow Gardens	LP	Midland
Drake House Memorial Museum	LP	Breckenridge
East Jordan Portside Art and Historical Museum	LP	East Jordan
Eaton County's Museum at Courthouse Square	LP	Charlotte
Edwardsburg Museum	LP	Edwardsburg
Elk Rapids Area Historical Museum	LP	Elk Rapids
Empire Area Museum Complex	LP	Empire
Engadine Historical Museum	UP	Engadine

Evart Public Library Museum	LP	Evart
Father Marquette National Memorial	UP	St. Ignace
Farwell Area Historical Museum	LP	Farwell
Fayette Historic Townsite	UP	Garden
Ferndale Historical Museum	LP	Ferndale
Fife Lake Historical Museum	LP	Fife Lake
Firebarn Museum	LP	Lake Ann
Fire Barn Museum	LP	Muskegon
Fire History Hall	LP	Hanover
Flat Rock Historical Museum	LP	Flat Rock
Florence B. Dearing Museum	LP	Hartland
Floyd and Mary Haight Archives	LP	Dearborn
Flushing Area Museum and Cultural Center	LP	Flushing
Ford Rouge Factory Tour	LP	Dearborn
Fort Mackinac	UP	Mackinac Island
Fort Wilkins Historic Complex	UP	Copper Harbor
Forty Mile Point Lighthouse	LP	Rogers City
Frankenmuth Historical Museum	LP	Frankenmuth
Franklin Historical Museum	LP	Franklin
Friends of the Thumb Octagon Barn	LP	Gagetown
Galesburg Historical Museum	LP	Galesburg
Gallimore Boarding House	LP	Roscommon
G.A.R. Hall	LP	Marshall
Gardener House Museum	LP	Albion
Garden City Historical Museum	LP	Garden City
Garden Peninsula Historical Museum	UP	Garden
Gerald R. Ford Presidential Library	LP	Ann Arbor
Gerald R. Ford Presidential Museum	LP	Grand Rapids
Gilmore Car Museum	LP	Hickory Corners
Gladwin County Historic Village	LP	Gladwin
Grand Blanc Heritage Association Museum	LP	Grand Blanc
Grand Ledge Museum	LP	Grand Ledge
Grand Ledge Opera House	LP	Grand Ledge
Grand Rapids Public Library History Collections	LP	Grand Rapids
Grand Traverse Heritage Center	LP	Traverse City
Grandville Historical Commission Museum	LP	Grandville
Greenfield Village	LP	Dearborn
Green Oak Township Heritage Museum	LP	South Lyon
Grosse Ile Light	LP	Grosse Ile
Hack House Museum	LP	Milan
Hackley and Hume Historic Site	LP	Muskegon
Hadley House Museum	LP	Holly
Hamburg Historical Museum	LP	Hamburg
Hanover-Horton Museum	LP	Hanover
Harbor House Museum	UP	Crystal Falls
Harbor Springs History Museum	LP	Harbor Springs
Harsha House Museum	LP	Charlevoix
Hart Historic District	LP	Hart
Hartwick Pines Logging Museum	LP	Grayling
Henry Ford	LP	Dearborn
Heritage Battle Creek	LP	Battle Creek
Heritage House Farm Museum	LP	Essexville

Heritage Museum	UP	Menominee
Heritage Museum and Cultural Center	LP	St. Joseph
Heritage Park	LP	Hanover
Heritage Park	LP	Midland
Hillsdale County Museum	LP	Hillsdale
Historic Adventist Village	LP	Battle Creek
Historical Association of South Haven	LP	South Haven
Historical Museum of Bay County	LP	Bay City
Historic Charlton Park Village	LP	Hastings
Historic Downtown Mackinac	UP	Mackinac Island
Historic Hanover School	LP	Hanover
Historic Mill Creek Discovery Park	LP	Mackinaw City
Historic Waterford Village	LP	Waterford
Historic White Pine Village	LP	Ludington
History Center at Courthouse Square	LP	Berrien Springs
Holland Museum	LP	Holland
Holocaust Memorial Center	LP	Farmington Hills
Honolulu House	LP	Marshall
Houghton County Museum	UP	Lake Linden
Houghton Lake Area Historical Village	LP	Prudenville
Howell Depot Museum	LP	Howell
Huron Lightship	LP	Port Huron
Imlay City Historical Museum	LP	Imlay City
Ionia County Museum	LP	Ionia
Iron County Historical Museum	UP	Caspian
Iron Mountain Iron Mine	UP	Vulcan
IXL Historical Museum	UP	Hermansville
Jarvis Stone School	LP	Salem
Jenison Historical Museum	LP	Jenison
Jim Crow Museum of Racist Memorabilia	LP	Big Rapids
John Schneider Blacksmith Shop Museum	LP	Manchester
Joint Archives of Holland	LP	Holland
Kalamazoo Valley Museum	LP	Kalamazoo
Kaleva Bottle House Museum	LP	Kaleva
Kalkaska County Museum	LP	Kalkaska
Kelley-Fisk Farm	LP	White Lake
Kempf House Museum	LP	Ann Arbor
Keweenaw County Historical Society Museums	UP	Eagle Harbor
Keweenaw National Historical Park	UP	Calumet
Kinross Heritage Park	UP	Kinross
Knowles Historical Museum	LP	Central Lake
Lakeshore Museum Center	LP	Muskegon
Lapeer Museum	LP	Lapeer
Leelanau Historical Museum	LP	Leland
Les Cheneaux Historical and Maritime Museums	UP	Cedarville
LeSault de Ste. Marie (Sault Historic Sites)	UP	Sault Ste. Marie
Liberty Hyde Bailey Museum	LP	South Haven
Library of Michigan	LP	Lansing
Lightkeeper's House Museum	UP	Grand Marais
Lincoln Park Historical Museum	LP	Lincoln Park
Loren Andrus Octagon House	LP	Washington
Lovells Township Historical Society Museums	LP	Grayling

Lowell Area Historical Museum	LP	Lowell
Luce County Historical Museum	UP	Newberry
Lyon Schoolhouse Memorial Museum	LP	Brighton
Mackinac Island State Park	UP	Mackinac Island
Mackinac State Historic Parks	LP	Mackinaw City
Mackinaw Area Historic Village	LP	Mackinaw City
Mann House	LP	Concord
Marilla Museum and Pioneer Place	LP	Mesick
Marine City Pride and Heritage Museum	LP	Marine City
Marquette Regional History Center	UP	Marquette
Mary's City of David	LP	Benton Harbor
Mason Area Historical Museum	LP	Mason
McFadden-Ross House	LP	Dearborn
McKenzie One-Room School	LP	Atlanta
Mecosta County Historical Society Museum	LP	Big Rapids
Menominee Range Museum	UP	Iron Mountain
Meridian Historical Village	LP	Okemos
Michigamme Museum	UP	Michigamme
Michigan Central Railroad Museum	LP	Grosse Ile
Michigan Flywheelers Museum	LP	South Haven
Michigan Historical Center	LP	Lansing
Michigan Iron Industry Museum	UP	Negaunee
Michigan Railroad History	LP	Durand
Michigan State University Museum	LP	East Lansing
Michigan Transit Museum	LP	Mount Clemens
Michigan Women's Historical Center and Hall of Fame	LP	Lansing
Milford Historical Museum	LP	Milford
Mill Race Village	LP	Northville
Missaukee County Museum	LP	Lake City
Montague Museum	LP	Montague
Montrose Historical and Pioneer Telephone Museum	LP	Montrose
Motown Museum	LP	Detroit
Museum of Cultural and Natural History	LP	Mount Pleasant
Museum on Main Street	LP	Ann Arbor
Museum Ship Valley Camp	UP	Sault Ste. Marie
Music House Museum	LP	Acme
Muskegon Heritage Museum	LP	Muskegon
Naval Airstation Grosse Ile	LP	Grosse Ile
New Presque Isle Lighthouse	LP	Presque Isle
Newton House	LP	Decatur
North Berrien Historical Museum	LP	Coloma
Northeast Oakland Historical Society	LP	Oxford
North Sidney Church and Cemetery	LP	Sidney
Norwegian Lutheran Church	UP	Calumet
Oceana County Historical and Genealogical Society Research Library and Headquarters	LP	Hart
Oceana Historical Park and Museum	LP	Mears
Ogemaw Genealogical and Historical Society Museum	LP	West Branch
Old Depot Museum	UP	Ironwood

Old Jail Museum	LP	Allegan
Old Mackinac Point Lighthouse	LP	Mackinaw City
Old Mission Peninsula Historical Society	LP	Old Mission
Old Post Office Museum and Memorial Rose Garden	UP	Grand Marais
Old Presque Isle Lighthouse	LP	Presque Isle
Old Sebewaing Township Hall	LP	Sebewaing
Olive Township Museum	LP	Holland
Ontonagon Historical Museum	UP	Ontonagon
Ontonagon Lighthouse	UP	Ontonagon
Orchard Lake Museum	LP	Orchard Lake
Otsego Area Historical Museum	LP	Otsego
Otsego County Historical Museum	LP	Gaylord
Ovid Historical Society Museum	LP	Ovid
Paine-Gilliam-Scott Museum	LP	St. Johns
Painesdale Mine and Shaft	UP	Painesdale
Pentwater Historical Museum	LP	Pentwater
Pickford Area Historical Society Museum	UP	Pickford
Pickle Barrell House Museum and Historic Iris Garden	UP	Grand Marais
Pine Grove Museum/Gov. Moses Wisner Home	LP	Pontiac
Plank Road Museum	LP	Breckenridge
Plymouth Historical Museum	LP	Plymouth
Port Huron Museum	LP	Port Huron
Post Street Archives	LP	Midland
Presque Isle County Historical Museum	LP	Rogers City
Presque Isle Township Museum	LP	Presque Isle
Provencal-Weir House	LP	Grosse Pt. Farms
Public Museum of Grand Rapids	LP	Grand Rapids
Putnam-Cloud Tower House	LP	Omena
Quincy Mine Hoist	UP	Hancock
Rathbone School	UP	Eagle Harbor
Rentschler Farm Museum	LP	Saline
R. E. Olds Transportation Museum	LP	Lansing
Richard and Jane Manoogian Mackinac Art Museum	UP	Mackinac Island
River of History Museum	UP	Sault Ste. Marie
Rochester Hills Museum at Van Hoosen Farm	LP	Rochester Hills
Rockford Area Historical Museum	LP	Rockford
Rockland Township Historical Museum	UP	Rockland
Romeo Arts and Archives Center	LP	Romeo
Royal Oak Historical Society Museum	LP	Royal Oak
S.S. City of Milwaukee	LP	Manistee
St. Clair Historical Museum	LP	St. Clair
St. Louis Historic Park	LP	St. Louis
Saginaw Railway Museum	LP	Saginaw
Saline Depot Museum	LP	Saline
Samuel Adams Historical Museum	LP	New Boston
Sanford Centennial Museum	LP	Sanford
Sanilac County Historic Village and Museum	LP	Lexington
Saugatuck-Douglas Historical Museum	LP	Douglas
Schoolcraft County Historical Park	UP	Manistique

Scolnik House of the Depression Era	LP	Muskegon
Sebewaing Area Historical Society	LP	Sebewaing
Selinsky-Green Farmhouse Museum	LP	St. Clair Shores
Settlers House Museum	LP	Holland
Shepherd Area Historical Society Museum	LP	Shepherd
Shiawassee County Museum	LP	Owosso
Shrine of the Snowshoe Priest	UP	L'Anse
Southerland-Wilson Farm Museum	LP	Ann Arbor
Southwestern Michigan College Museum	LP	Dowagiac
Steiner Museum	LP	Fairview
Sturgeon Point Lighthouse and Museum	LP	Harrisville
Sturgis Historical Society	LP	Sturgis
Tahquamenon Logging Museum	UP	Newberry
Tawas Point Lighthouse	LP	East Tawas
Taylor Heritage Park	LP	Taylor
Tecumseh Area Historical Society Museum	LP	Tecumseh
Thomas Edison Depot Museum	LP	Port Huron
Tower of History	UP	Sault Ste. Marie
Trenton Historical Museum	LP	Trenton
Tri-Cities Historical Museum	LP	Grand Haven
Turner-Dodge House	LP	Lansing
Ukrainian American Archives and Museum	LP	Hamtramck
Upton House	LP	Sterling Heights
U.S. Coast Guard Cutter Bramble	LP	Port Huron
U.S. Land Office	LP	White Pigeon
U.S. Ski and Snowboard Hall of Fame	UP	Ishpeming
Van Buren County Historical Society Museum	LP	Hartford
Vicksburg Depot Museum	LP	Vicksburg
Voigt House Victorian Museum	LP	Grand Rapids
Wakefield Museum	UP	Wakefield
Walker Tavern Historic Complex	LP	Brooklyn
Warren Historical Gallery	LP	Warren
Washington Historical Museum	LP	Washington
Waterloo Farm Museum	LP	Grass Lake
Water Street Historic Block	UP	Sault Ste. Marie
Watrousville Museum	LP	Caro
Wellington Farm Park	LP	Grayling
Wexford County Historical Society	LP	Cadillac
Whaley House Museum	LP	Flint
Wheels of History Museum Train	UP	Brimley
Whistlestop Depot	LP	Grass Lake
White Rock School Museum	LP	Harbor Beach
Will Carleton Poorhouse Museum	LP	Hillsdale
William G. Thomson House Museum and Gardens	LP	Hudson
William L. Clements Library	LP	Ann Arbor
Witch's Hat Historic Village and Museum	LP	South Lyon
Wyandotte Historical Museum	LP	Wyandotte
Yankee Air Force Museum Wurtsmith Division	LP	Oscoda
Yankee Air Museum	LP	Ypsilanti
Zeeland Historical Museum	LP	Zeeland

MICHIGAN
H I S T O R Y

Michigan History is our state's popular-history publication. Edited for entertainment as much as education, it features stories of all kinds from Michigan's colorful past. Within its pages, you'll learn about logging, mining, manufacturing, and military history as well as art, architecture, music, sports, shipwrecks, and more.

Engaging Features

Among the valued features in every issue are "Remember the Time," a reader-written reminiscence; "Communiqués," a news section highlighting historical happenings throughout the state; and "Conversations," an informative interview with a prominent professional working to preserve Michigan's history.

Informative Articles

A team of talented contributors generates the magazine's historical content—up to eight articles per issue. Samples of past issue content may be found at www.hsmichigan.org.

Full-Color Graphics

Each issue is filled with colorful photographs, maps, and engravings collected from museums and archives around the state and the country. Besides being historically accurate, these images bring each story to life.

Timely Delivery

Michigan History is distributed six times a year, in January, March, May, July, September, and November. As a subscriber, you'll receive the publication weeks before it's available on the newsstand.

Subscribe to
MICHIGAN HISTORY *magazine!*

Complete this form and mail or fax to:

Michigan History Magazine
Historical Society of Michigan
5815 Executive Drive, Lansing, MI 48911
Fax: (517) 324-4370

☐ I'm ready to order a one-year subscription $19.95
☐ I'd like to order a discounted two-year subscription $34.95

_____

Name (please print)

_____

Address

_____

City, State, Zip:

_____

Telephone

Payment
☐ Check payable to Michigan History Magazine
☐ Credit card: Visa, Discover, MasterCard, AMEX

_____

Account/Card Number

_____

Exp. Date (mm/yy)   CVV Code

_____

Signature

_____

Name as it appears on card

For faster service, call (800) 366-3703 and charge to
Visa, Discover, MasterCard, or American Express.

The

Historical

Society

of

Michigan

Membership Information

PUBLICATIONS

All members receive our quarterly magazine, the *Chronicle,* which includes the *Michigan Teacher* three times per year.

Upgrade to Regular membership to get the *Michigan Historical Review*, the only scholarly journal focused on Michigan's history.

Enhance either Basic or Regular membership with HSM's *Michigan History* magazine at significant savings.

Other publications include our triennial *Michigan History Directory* that provides detailed listings for over 800 historical organizations statewide and the *Historic Michigan Travel Guide,* also published triennially.

CONFERENCES

HSM sponsors four annual conferences including the State History Conference, Upper Peninsula History Conference, Mulling Over Michigan, and Michigan in Perspective: the Local History Conference.

Conferences include:
- Workshops and tours
- Keynotes and breakout sessions
- Awards
- Banquets and entertainment
- Networking and more!

HSM members receive a discount on conference registration fees and hotel rates.

WORKSHOPS

In addition to workshop opportunities at the annual conferences, HSM also sponsors stand-alone workshops such as Basic Archives, Disaster Planning, and more. Members receive information on training events as soon as it becomes available and are eligible for significant registration discounts.

Milestone plaques & Centennial Farms

HSM offers Milestone Award cast-metal plaques celebrating anniversaries between 50 and 200 years for businesses and Organizations. We also operate the Centennial Farms program for Michigan.

Networking

Participate in a statewide network dedicated to connecting people with the resources they need through meetings, workshops, publications, a speakers bureau, and more.

Awards

- The State History Awards—including the Lifetime Achievement Award—are presented at the State Conference each fall.
- The Charles Follo Award (for individuals) and the Superior Award (for organizations) are both awarded at the Upper Peninsula History conference in the summer.

Local support

HSM provides extensive support to local historical organizations. Services include:

- Formation, programming, and best practices
- Training and workshops
- Programs featured on an online Calendar of Events
- Website creation and support
- Listing in the *Michigan History Directory*
- Statewide exposure and networking

EDUCATIONAL PROGRAMS

Michigan History Day

Michigan History Day is our flagship educational activity and a part of the National History Day program.

History Day promotes history education for students in 4th through 12th grade and encourages them to participate in a series of local, regional, and state competitions by creating exhibits, documentaries, papers, websites, or performances. This program develops critical thinking skills, research abilities, literacy, and other scholarship attributes. Winners advance to national finals held at the University of Maryland each June.

Mulling Over Michigan

Held each fall, Mulling Over Michigan is an HSM conference focused on educators who teach Michigan's history in the classroom and others who provide services to educators including museums.

The conference increases the quality and quantity of Michigan state and local history teaching and promotes its incorporation into the social studies curricula.

Multiple breakouts are offered, topics covered change annually, and exhibitors present resources for teaching Michigan history.

Join HSM!

To join, call toll-free (800) 692-1828 or
complete this form and mail or fax to:
Historical Society of Michigan
5815 Executive Drive, Lansing, MI 48911
Fax: (517) 324-4370
You may also join online at
www.hsmichigan.org.

_____

Name (please print)

_____

Address

_____

City, State, Zip:

_____

Telephone

_____

E-mail*

** HSM protects your privacy. Your e-mail will be used for HSM member
communications only.*

Membership

□ Basic (includes the *Chronicle* magazine) $25
□ Regular (adds the *Michigan Historical Review* journal) $35
□ Historical Organization (annual budget of less than $25,000) $35
□ Museum or Library (annual budget of more than $25,000) $50

**Enhanced membership adds *Michigan History* magazine for
only $15 more (nearly $5 off the subscription price):**

    □ Enhanced Basic $40
    □ Enhanced Regular or Historical Society $50
    □ Enhanced Museum or Library $65

For *Michigan History* magazine subscription only, see page 121.

Payment
□ Check payable to the Historical Society of Michigan
□ Credit card: Visa, Discover, MasterCard, AMEX

_____

Account/Card Number

_____

Exp. Date (mm/yy)   CVV Code

_____

Signature

The Historical Society of Michigan

The Historical Society of Michigan is an educational non-profit that promotes Michigan history through publications, conferences, educational programs, and services to local historical organizations statewide. Founded in 1828 by Governor Lewis Cass and explorer Henry Schoolcraft, the Society is Michigan's oldest cultural institution and sponsors annual conferences including the State History Conference, Upper Peninsula History Conference, Michigan in Perspective: the Local History Conference, and Mulling Over Michigan. It publishes the quarterly magazine the *Chronicle* and the bi-monthly *Michigan History* magazine, the *Historic Michigan Travel Guide*, the *Michigan History Directory*, and the *Michigan Historical Review* (in cooperation with Central Michigan University). Educational programs include Michigan History Day (National History Day in Michigan), educator training, and more. The Society also provides an array of support services, training, and outreach for over 800 local historical organizations in Michigan.

Contact us at:

The Historical Society of Michigan
5815 Executive Drive
Lansing, MI 48911

Toll-free: (800) 692-1828
Fax: (517) 324-4370

Or join us online at:
www.hsmichigan.org